THE GROWTH OF
Reading

E D I T E D   B Y
Malcolm Petyt

ALAN SUTTON

First published in the United Kingdom in 1993 by
Alan Sutton Publishing Limited
Phoenix Mill · Far Thrupp · Stroud · Gloucestershire

First published in the United States of America in 1993 by
Alan Sutton Publishing Inc · 83 Washington Street · Dover · NH 03820

British Library Cataloguing in Publication Data

Growth of Reading
   1. Petyt, Malcolm
   1. Title
   942.293

ISBN 0-7509-0330-9

Typeset in 10/14 Plantin Light.
Typesetting and origination by
Alan Sutton Publishing Limited.
Printed and bound in Great Britain by
Redwood Books, Trowbridge.

THE GROWTH OF
Reading

Contents

List of Contributors   vi

Acknowledgements   vii

Introduction   ix

1   Reading in Saxon and Danish Times   1

2   Reading Abbey and the Medieval Town   31

3   Reading in the Sixteenth and Seventeenth Centuries   56

4   Reading in the Eighteenth Century and Victorian Times   83

Bibliography   108

Index   110

Contributors

Text written by:

C.F. SLADE BA PhD FRHistS FSA, formerly Reader in History and later Head of the Department of Archaeology, University of Reading

B.R. KEMP BA PhD FRHistS FSA, Professor of History, University of Reading

J.A. DILS BA CertEd, Extramural Lecturer and Staff Tutor in History, Department of Extended Education, University of Reading

T.A.B. CORLEY MA, formerly Senior Lecturer in Economics, University of Reading

Text edited by:

K.M. PETYT MA PhD DiP PSA FRSA, Head of the Department of Extended Education, University of Reading

Illustrations collected by:

C.L. CRAM MA AMA FSA, Principal Keeper of Collections and Keeper of Archaeology, Reading Museum and Art Gallery

Acknowledgements

Grateful acknowledgement for permission to reproduce illustrations is made to the following individuals and institutions, with whom the copyright or reproduction rights reside. Illustrations are listed by page number:

The Ashmolean Museum, Oxford, 8, 22; the Master and Scholars of Balliol College, Oxford, 45 (top); Berkshire Record Office for Reading Borough Council, 59; The Bodleian Library, Oxford, 46; The British Library, London, 43, 80; Mrs H.S. Brock, 97; Niall Cook, 2, 6, 9, 32, 105; T.A.B. Corley, 94 (top and bottom), 98 (top and bottom), 99, 100; the Master and Fellows of Corpus Christi College, Cambridge, 16; Courage (Central) Limited, 91, 93; The Conway Library, The Courtauld Institute of Art, London, 38, 41; Simon Eager, 40 (left and right); Jonathan Farmer, 15 (top and bottom), 23, 24, 25, 26; The Dean and Chapter of Hereford Cathedral, 45 (bottom); Brian Kemp, 54 (bottom); Reading Museum and Art Gallery, 12, 15 (top and bottom), 23, 24, 25, 26, 34, 35, 37, 38, 41, 42, 47, 49, 53, 54 (top), 75, 77 (top and bottom), 79, 84, 89; Reading Public Library, 87; the vicar of St Laurence's church, Reading, 58; The Dean and Chapter of Salisbury Cathedral, 40 (left); Suttons Seeds Limited, 96, 102; The Trust for Wessex Archaeology Limited, 5, 42, 44; University of Reading Archives, 101 (top and bottom), 104 (top and bottom); The Dean and Chapter of Westminster Abbey, 40 (right).

Introduction

In 1990 two major institutions in Reading collaborated to mount the first of what was to become an annual series of 'Town Hall Lectures'. Using the facilities of the newly refurbished Town Hall (one of Reading's finest buildings, designed by the town's most distinguished architect, Alfred Waterhouse), the Department of Extended Education at the University of Reading and the Reading Museum and Art Gallery organized a series of lectures about the history of the town.

The lectures were well attended, and in the following years further series were arranged, which also drew on the resources of both the university and the museum. The enthusiasm for the 'Town Hall Lectures' led to the proposal that some of them should be made available in more permanent form. A publisher was found, and this volume presents four lectures from the first series, which trace the history of Reading from its earliest times to the beginning of the twentieth century.

The authors are all senior members of the university, and well known in the area for their knowledge and enthusiasm about various aspects of the history of the town. Cecil Slade was for many years a member of the Department of History, and later was the first head of the Department of Archaeology. His lecture dealt with the development of the town in Saxon and Danish times, including its occupation by the Danes and the opposition led by Alfred the Great. Brian Kemp is a distinguished medievalist in the Department of History. He covered the period of the mighty Reading Abbey, a building probably as large as Salisbury Cathedral, which was founded by Henry I and became a centre of devotion to St James. Joan Dils is a member of the Extramural Section of the Department of Extended Education, and she is well known in adult education circles. Her lecture described Reading in the sixteenth and seventeenth centuries, and showed clearly why her classes on local history have been so popular with the public of Reading. The fourth lecture was by Tony Corley of the Department of Economics, who has worked extensively on the industrial and commercial history of the town. He discussed developments in the two centuries when Reading grew into an industrial centre of regional importance, particularly associated with the production of biscuits, seeds and beer, with many other lesser known but important businesses also developing because of Reading's excellent communications by road, water and rail.

In preparing this volume for publication it has been my enjoyable duty as editor to recast the four lectures in a form more appropriate for a book. I have also provided an index of subjects. The collaboration between the two sponsoring institutions has continued in that Leslie Cram of the Reading Museum and Art Gallery has been responsible for gathering the illustrations. The timing of the publication of this book is particularly apt in that the museum reopened in September 1993 after extensive refurbishment by the Reading Borough Council. Both of us appreciate the cooperation we have received from the authors and the publishers.

Malcolm Petyt
University of Reading
October 1993

1

Reading in Saxon and Danish Times

CECIL SLADE

For a very long time before the coming of the Saxons, small groups of people had lived around, and possibly in, the area that was to become the town of Reading (not the modern town area, but the very much smaller one of earlier times). However, there seems to have been no concentration of population in any one location. In Roman times, for example, there appears to have been only a scatter of small rural settlements, almost certainly administered from Silchester, the nearest important town. Our evidence comes from many chance finds, although few of these are from the area of Reading itself; but, allowing for the fact that later building would tend to destroy the flimsy foundations of a Romano-British village, the evidence does not indicate any concentrated settlement here.

Why was there no concentration of population? After all, the site had considerable advantages. It consisted of well-drained gravel overlying chalk, with the top of the ridge some thirty feet above the Thames and so free from flooding. The middle of the ridge was cut by the Kennet, which offered communication westward and, together with its branches, provided a copious water supply. Moreover, the Thames, joined by the Kennet just east of Reading, offered communication with Londinium, the main town of Roman Britain. What communication was like by land is not so clear, but the Oxford Road is supposed to represent an ancient trackway, and the crossing of the Thames at Caversham is also thought to go back to ancient times.

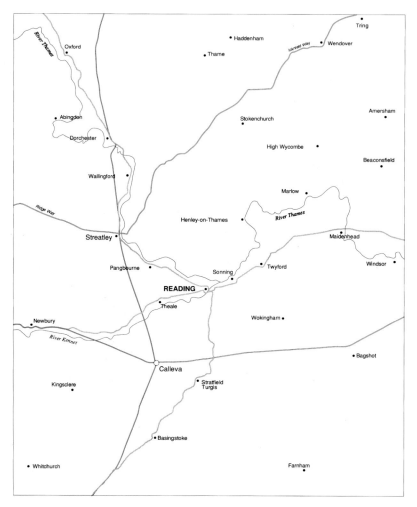

The geographical position of Reading and the main communication routes in the Roman and Saxon periods. The Roman roads converged on the Roman town of Calleva, while the Saxon routes met at Reading

So in these early times there was apparently a site that was very thinly occupied, but which had a huge potential for increased settlement. It may have had a name but, if so, it has vanished.

The fifth century AD is a very confused period, especially for the historian of Britain. For much of that century Roman administration continued to function, even if rather crudely, with methods which included the use of Germans, perhaps as hired troops, perhaps as soldier-settlers with the emphasis on the settler role. But increasingly as the fifth century wore on, that administration broke down in the face of larger bands of invaders entering the country. There were some early and comparatively large Saxon settlements in the area later to be known as North Berkshire, but more relevant to our subject are a number of early Germanic cemeteries along the south bank of the middle Thames. It has been suggested that these might indicate forward defences, manned by Germans and organized by a late Roman authority based at Silchester. One of these cemeteries, a small one, is just to the east of Kennet mouth. There was another small cemetery near the later Jack of Both Sides inn, and an early cremation vessel was found near Southcote. No habitation sites have been discovered either at these locations or within the town's early area. On the site of the later abbey were found a few sherds, animal bones and small metal objects, which might hint at a settlement nearby, and a few sherds turned up near Crane Wharf. Some of the few weapons and other objects found in scattered locations belong to this early period. These include an identifiable Merovingian horse-bit from the Thames and a shield boss from the Battle area, but the axes and spearheads which have been discovered come from a wide range of periods, and some of the pottery is clearly of a later date.

However imprecise the evidence, a named settlement did develop on this spot, although the name itself is the only early proof we have. The first surviving writing of the name occurs around AD 900, but the name itself is from an earlier time. Place-name studies are a minefield, and the non-expert is well advised to steer clear of

Objects discovered during archaeological excavations in 1891 at the Dreadnought pagan Saxon cemetery near Kennet mouth

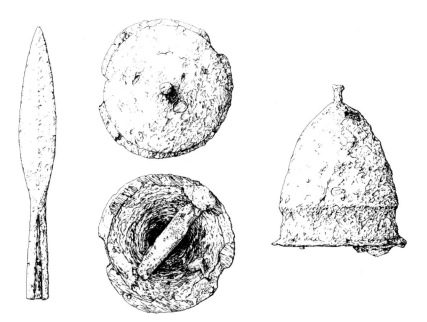

Shield boss and spear from excavations in 1985 of the pagan Saxon cemetery at Burghfield

controversy, but at present there is no dispute that this particular name was formed from a group name combined with a personal name or nickname which had long been obsolete by AD 900. The individual's name was *Reada*, literally 'the Red', and it was his people the *Readingas*, the followers of Reada, who bequeathed their name to this place.

Beyond this all is guesswork. For instance, did Reada come to Britain, or was he an ancestral figure who had lived long before? Did he or a descendant lead a group who were looking to settle, or was he a warlord who imposed his authority, peacefully or brutally, on the people already there? Was this leader freelancing, or was he part of a larger organization? All we can safely say is that at some time in the sixth century a recognizable group, the *Readingas*, became established in an area some seven miles across (the later hundred of Reading,

The hundred of Reading as it was in 1086 recorded in Domesday Book, probably little changed then from its extent over the previous five hundred years

which included Pangbourne and Theale). There is some query as to where the focus of this territory was (i.e. the 'original' Reading), for the Reading known to history is near the boundary of the area, whereas it would seem more natural for the original headquarters to have been closer to the centre. At any rate, at some time the group name became connected with a settlement where Reading now stands.

So now we have a settlement, probably inhabited by a mixture of indigenous population and newcomers, with the language and way of life of the latter predominating. These newcomers seem to have been Saxons, coming from western Germany or the Low Countries, but what route did they take? There are three main possibilities: from the Wash down the Icknield Way; by boat up the Thames; or from the south coast. Again we only have hints from archaeology and place-names to guide us, but it seems very possible that the eastern part of what later became Berkshire has much more in common with Surrey than with west Berkshire, and that it was settled from that direction. It has even been suggested that the early kingdom of the Middle Saxons, which included Surrey, may have included this eastern part of Berkshire.

Since the matter of counties has been raised, this is a convenient point at which to consider the place of Reading within a larger grouping. If there was a Middle Saxon kingdom, this had a very short life, and from the time for which definite information is available the area of Reading was under the rule of the kings of Wessex, the West Saxons. The early years must have been difficult, with two rival dynasties fighting: one was based in the Thames Valley, the other in Winchester, with the latter ultimately triumphing. The kings of Wessex continued to hold the area and, incidentally, to found Abingdon Abbey, but by the late seventh century the kings of Mercia, the great Midland kingdom, had extended their authority to the north bank of the Thames, and after 726 King Æthelbald of Mercia exercised authority even south of the river. For twenty years after his murder in 759 the area was again under the kings of Wessex, but after the battle of Bensington (779) King Offa of Mercia controlled it. This situation continued even after the Battle of Ellandune in 825, won by King Egbert of Wessex. Though Surrey and areas further east then came under his power, this area remained under Mercian control until the mid-840s. In 849, however, Alfred, youngest son of the West Saxon King Æthelwulf, was born in Wantage in north Berkshire, but the same Mercian *ealdorman* (the king's representative) continued to govern the county, although now serving the West Saxon king, until 870.

What about Berkshire, which became Reading's county? It is first mentioned in 860 and appears to be unique in that it is not named after people (like Somerset), nor after its main town (like Yorkshire). If it had been named after a town it would have been

The head of King
Alfred on a silver
penny

Wallingfordshire, certainly not Readingshire. It seems, as far as the
Saxons were concerned, to have been an artificial creation produced
by putting together two areas – one linked with the east and the other
with connections west or even north-west – and naming the result
after an obscure wood (*Bearroc*) in the western part. This name is a
Celtic word, meaning 'hilly'. For the 200–250 years from the time
Berkshire is first mentioned, Reading came under its control, the
settlement being within the authority of the ealdorman in charge of
Berkshire.

   Whether changes of kingdom had any effect on Reading we do not
know, but as the powers of kings were very limited in this period it is
probable that such changes made little difference. In any case the
whole country spoke dialects of the same language, and civilization,
economic life, political ideas, law and religion were essentially the
same over the greater part of England – and ealdorman Æthelwulf

had no difficulty in changing his allegiance. There could be trouble if military affairs impinged directly on a settlement, but armies were small and mainly short-lived, and we certainly hear nothing of any battles fought in this area. So let us assume that life continued fairly normally, and glance briefly at the way of life in the Reading area in this early and middle Saxon period.

The settlement here was one of a number in the area which later became the manor of Reading. Like the others, the Reading settlement would have been a small village surrounded by its cultivated fields, for the people would have had to feed themselves. There would probably have been a couple of common fields for

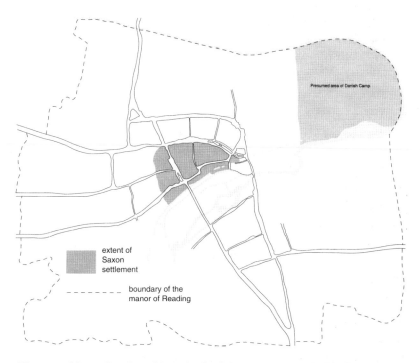

Presumed area of Danish Camp

extent of
Saxon
settlement

boundary of the
manor of Reading

The area of Saxon Reading with the lands of the manor around it. The Danish camp of 870 was said, in Asser's 'Life of Alfred', to have been between the Kennet and the Thames, and protected by a rampart arable crops, possibly to both the north and the south, with meadow land along the Thames. The river, though of course uncontrolled as yet by locks, was useful for transport, since travel by land was slow and expensive, but it was to be many centuries before built-up Reading actually extended as far as the Thames and the mouth of the Kennet. It was in fact the Kennet, with its various channels, which was of most use to Reading. The settlement was clustered along it; its water was used for drinking, washing, tanning and so forth; and the main stream was a line of communication with places to the west. Judging by the activity in later times, it was probably also a place for dumping rubbish.

Rivers are, of course, more or less fixed features, but roads can change. At some stage two important roads which formerly crossed at Silchester came to do so at Reading. One was the north-south road from Southampton and Winchester to Wallingford, Oxford and the Midlands, with a less important branch going north-east; the other was the east-west road from London to Bath.

Why this movement in the lines of communication came about we do not know. Possibly it was because Reading was there, or perhaps it was this change that helped to bring Reading into existence. We shall never know when it happened or why: it is easy to produce theories, but nothing can be proved. Bridges, fords, politics, economics or any other factors are all guesses, but it is helpful to remember that a road at this time was no more than a well-travelled route. Roman roads were, of course, well constructed and had definite edges, but other so-called roads had no proper surfaces and no obvious borders: if the puddles were bad, travellers walked or rode to either side. There was little that the peasant cultivators of fields could do about this; in any case, areas of cultivation were much less extensive than later. So perhaps the change of route developed gradually; people knew where they were heading, but the actual line of travel was not particularly important.

Whatever the reason, the two roads came together at what was later to be Horn Street, and they separated again at what we know as Gun

Street and the Butts, and it was at this latter point that the earliest market and church developed. Thus Reading came to be focused on the road junctions. It has been suggested that the original site of the settlement may have been in the defensive angle between the two rivers; if this were so, the move downhill to the road junction would represent a major development in the history of the town.

The people living in Reading would have been a rather mixed collection, for over the years there must have been intermarriage between Saxons and the pre-Saxon inhabitants of the area. The period up to about 870 seems to have seen a rise in population despite visitations of the plague, but a settlement such as this one would probably not exceed 100 or 150 inhabitants at the best of times. Life would seem to us to have been nasty, brutish and short, with a monotonous diet, periodic food shortages, primitive medical care, scratchy clothing (which was normally also rather dirty and flea-infested) and great dependence on the weather. Houses were built of wood or wattle and daub, with thatched roofs and earth floors. They would have had just one main room and perhaps some subsidiary accommodation for animals. Better houses would have been bigger and offered slightly more privacy, but there cannot have been many of these in Reading. Most people in this small community would have been related in some way, and the community would have provided for its weaker members, the young and the old. Not that there were many old people: there were too many natural and man-made impediments to longevity, although some did attain the ripe old age of fifty. There would have been a number of children, but infant mortality was high, and far fewer than half would have survived to their teens.

Most inhabitants would have been free people (*ceorls*), but there would also have been a number of slaves, both male and female. This group was recruited from criminals, debtors and captives taken in war. The slaves had hard lives, but they enjoyed certain modest rights, and manumission was possible. A free man carried the

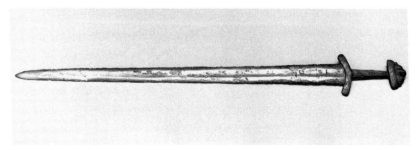

Only the elite wore the sword. This one was dredged from the Thames

standard weapon of Anglo-Saxon England, the spear, for only the élite wore swords. Among freemen there were various ranks, including *geburs* and *cotsetlas* who were lower on the social and economic scale than the ceorls. There had always been some form of dependence in a society where leaders, from the kings downwards, had their followers, but during this time there was also a growing territorial dependence: manorialism. As society became stabilized its leaders, *gesiths* or *thegns*, had to be supplied with the resources to meet their military and governmental obligations, and to maintain their position in society.

Kings of course needed the largest resources. Although their duties at this time were very limited compared with later, they were increasing. The king's income would have come from various sources, the steadiest of these being food rents – paid originally in kind but later in cash – from the inhabitants of the lands the king kept under his direct control. As a result of some unknown process, the large and wealthy manor of Reading was by 870 held by the king. What difference this made to the inhabitants is unclear. The king would have had some local representative, the *tun-gerefa*, to look after his interests, and he may not have been as harsh as a local lord. Perhaps the fact that it was a royal holding would have caused some hesitation before it was attacked or sacked. It is possible that the more important people of the locality gained easier access to the king, but for most inhabitants life would probably have been much as before. However, later times would show this status as a royal holding to have been of great significance in the development of Reading.

Another important factor was the coming of Christianity. How this reached the area is not clear: perhaps something had survived from Roman Britain. We do know that the Scottish Church, established in Iona, was active in the North and the Midlands, and that St Augustine's mission from Rome had arrived in Kent in 597. However, progress by the latter had been slow, and the area of Reading, on the border between kingdoms, probably had to await the coming of St Birinus, who around 634 established at Dorchester-on-Thames the headquarters from which he went out preaching. Later, when the area was under the control of Mercia, it came under the bishopric of Leicester; when under Wessex it fell within the bishopric of Winchester (to which Agilbert, the second bishop at Dorchester, had moved). But whoever the bishop was, he would have been an infrequent visitor, and to most people he would have been a shadowy figure.

Of much more immediate importance would have been the local clergy: development of the Church would depend on the desire of local people to become priests. There were probably comparatively few at first, and the organization would have had to develop downwards. First the bishop's church, the cathedral; then the 'mother church', with a group of itinerant clergy serving a district; then, spread over the next three centuries or so, the parish churches developed. It is probable that the area of Reading had one of the mother churches, for it was about the right size and was possibly already held by the king. Whether this original church was in the actual *vill* of Reading or elsewhere in the manor we do not know: it would have been a flimsy building, and no trace survives. But there may be an indication in the name of Minster Street, meaning the street leading to the minster or mother church.

The whole story of the conversion to Christianity is steeped in problems. The Church worked by getting the kings and the leading men on its side, so that bonds of loyalty would make their retainers follow suit. Sentiment varied during the seventh century: on the one hand we hear of kings relapsing into heathenism; on the other there were soon native bishops and saints. The pattern was probably much the same among the humbler folk: some for, some against, but the majority indifferent or vaguely puzzled. Heathenism may not have had much hold, and there is no evidence of heathen sites of worship in the area. But what the church feared and fulminated against was not straightforward heathenism, but rather a dark underworld of evil, containing malignant spirits, ghosts, dragons and the like. These were very real to people who lived close to a harsh nature and had no scientific explanation for natural phenomena. Spells, incantations and other heathen practices were employed as medicine, and there must have been many other nastier practices to which people turned when prayer appeared to be ineffective. But Christianity, even if in a rather superstitious form, did become the way of life for most people, and no doubt many of them grumbled about rendering Church *scot* (tax) and Easter offerings when they found that the clergy needed more than just piety to sustain them.

By the ninth century we can assume that there was a well-established, if modest, community in Reading. Life would have been essentially agricultural, but it is likely that communications were encouraging some trade, and we can safely postulate a market, perhaps held weekly, which would have served people beyond the immediate confines of the settlement. The church, probably a wattle and daub or wooden building, would likewise have served a wider area. Most of the inhabitants would have been legally free, though some would have been lower than others on the economic scale. But there would not have been much difference in standards of living, with housing, food, clothing, pottery (dark and rather thick) and the sparse furniture much the same for all the inhabitants. Many of the men would have had military obligations, though armies were small, and campaigns were brief and limited to the summer. They would

Stages in the growing of corn. Left to right: ploughing, sowing, harrowing and scaring off birds. From the Bayeux Tapestry

also have been obliged to attend local assemblies under the presidency of the royal representative. The law, as it affected most people, was customary law or folk law, although kings were issuing law codes which dealt with controversial matters or matters important to the running of their kingdoms.

To what extent the changes in rule over this area involved military actions we do not know. There was probably some disturbance, but even at the best of times life was rough and violent, so this was expected. Indeed, violence was probably less perturbing than the plague and pestilence, which were also common but had no obvious cause. Providing military disturbances did not lead to the loss of food supplies, things would not have been too serious, for accommodation could be rebuilt quickly.

In 870, however, the way of life in this modest community was badly interrupted, and for the first time Reading appears in written records. Conflict was endemic among the English kingdoms, which had been reduced in number to four during the ninth century, but for more than a generation a new and much more serious dimension had been added by the arrival of peoples from northern Europe, especially the Danes. Reasons for their coming included the lack of opportunities at home, loot, excitement and prestige, for the way of

Hunting with hunting horn and dogs. From the Bayeux Tapestry

Of the early documents that survive, the first to mention Reading (*Readingum*; bottom line) is the Anglo-Saxon Chronicle entry of *c.* AD 900. It records the year as 871 but the first events refer to Autumn 870. It reads: 'Her cuom se here to Readingum on Westseaxe' ('In this year the [Danish] army came to Reading in Wessex').

life in northern Europe was based on warfare and martial virtues. The softer and wealthier parts of Europe further south were wide open to these seaborne attackers, whose ships' crews were both rowers and fighting men: they came in fleets of two hundred or more ships, and served voluntarily under leaders of renown, campaigning during the summer and returning home with their booty for the winter. But in 866 there began a new and ominous phase, during which Danes (or Vikings) came as a coherent group to spend the summer looting and fighting (and overthrowing kingdoms), and then in the autumn moving into winter quarters in England.

By 870 the kingdoms of Northumbria and East Anglia lay at the Vikings' disposal, with their kings dead and their armies defeated, and the king of Mercia was reduced to buying peace, a practice which was later to be known as paying *Danegeld*. What the good folk of Reading felt about this we do not know, but news of events must have reached them, because Reading was on major lines of communication. Vikings had a great reputation for ferocity, and we hear elsewhere of prayers in churches for delivery from the fury of the Norsemen. However, the dwellers in Wessex had some reason for confidence: they would have known of the resounding victory in 838 by King Egbert of Wessex over Danes and Cornishmen at Hingston Down; men from Reading may have been with King Æthelwulf in 851 when he inflicted a bloody defeat on the Danes at Aclea in nearby Surrey;

and some were probably among the men of Berkshire, who, under their ealdorman Æthelwulf, joined with the Hampshire forces in around 861 to defeat the Danes, who had just stormed Winchester. Apparently, military superiority lay with the men of Wessex, and certainly the Danes, once they started staying in England over the winter, had given their attention to other kingdoms and kept away from Wessex. All the more then must the folk of Reading have felt shattered when the Danish army suddenly appeared there in the autumn of 870 and set up winter camp.

As noted above, the manor of Reading had by this time become a royal estate. However, it is unlikely that its modest rural prosperity would have attracted the attention of the Danes, so one wonders why they should have decided to come to Reading. The Danish army had previously established winter quarters in such important places as York, Nottingham and Thetford, with which Reading could not compare. A clue may lie in its location: the part of the settlement between the rivers was a defensive site; it was not far from the main parts of Wessex to the south and it offered an easy retreat across the river into Mercia, whose king had bought peace, in case the West Saxon king should again succeed against them in battle. So from the Danes' point of view Reading was a good site. But how did they come to find it? Coming from East Anglia they would have taken the Icknield Way. However, this leads to the Goring Gap, so if they deviated off the direct line to cross the river at Caversham, they must have done a certain amount of forward planning and reconnaissance.

At any rate the Danes did arrive, and after a week they had constructed a rampart between the Thames and the Kennet. It is likely that at this stage the structure was the minimum necessary to be effective (it could be improved at leisure during the winter), so a combination of the Danes and forced local labour could have constructed it in the time. But where was it? No traces have been identified, though archaeologists have been looking for it for a long time. If we estimate the army as numbering between three and five thousand, plus their horses, and suppose that they would not occupy areas likely to flood nor want to have to defend an unnecessarily large area, then we can imagine a defensive line starting at the mouth of the Holy Brook and running north to the Thames. This would be the shortest line; if more space was needed, then the starting point was probably nearer the later High Bridge.

It is doubtful whether many of the inhabitants would have remained voluntarily to watch all these developments. Any who did stay would soon have seen a Danish raiding party rushing back in disorder after being defeated at Englefield by ealdorman Æthelwulf. It is possible that men from Reading took part in this fight; it is also very likely that some were involved four days later when the king and his brother Alfred tried to storm the Danish camp but were bloodily repulsed. Another few days later they would have seen the culmination of a fighting retreat to Reading by the Danes after the battle of Ashdown. But during the remainder of that year and early in the following one there would have been less encouraging sights: victorious booty-laden Danes returning from battles at Basing, Meretun and Wilton, and from many unknown battles and innumerable smaller raids. The Danes, in fact, were gaining the ascendancy. In the spring they were reinforced by the arrival of a great summer army, composed of troops who had wintered at home and who perhaps came up the Thames. For the Saxons, however, misfortunes culminated in the death of their king soon after Easter of 871. His successor, Alfred, had no option but to buy peace and leave the Danes based in their Reading camp until the autumn, when they moved to London.

How did the dwellers in this modest settlement cope in this traumatic year? Once the Danes had left we can assume that the surviving inhabitants returned fairly quickly. To rebuild small wattle and daub houses would have been no great task nor, given the amount of timber around, would the rebuilding of more substantial wooden dwellings. We do not know what those returning would have

The hilt of a sword, possibly Danish.
This was found in Reading in 1831
near the presumed area of the Viking
encampment of 870, along with the
skeletons of a man and his horse

done about food: they must have brought some supplies with them, for with an undeveloped market and the stripping of the surrounding countryside by the Danes (whose men and horses would have consumed two to three thousand tons of meat and grain at the very least), there can have been little around to purchase. There was probably miscellaneous debris left in the Danish camp which would have been put to good purpose. Perhaps local folk utilized every scrap, for here lies the mystery: no archaeological evidence of this Danish occupation has ever been found. Items of discarded equipment must have been thrown away; objects must have been dropped and lost; and there must have been many deaths, for wounds would readily turn gangrenous. However, apart from one grave of a man and horse, and a ninth-century sword, possibly Danish, found on the site of the later GWR station in 1831, there is as little evidence of artefacts as there is of the defensive ditch.

Although we assume that the site was abandoned by its English inhabitants during the Danish occupation, it is only guesswork. After the early attack by the king's forces and the follow-up after Ashdown, we hear nothing of fighting in the neighbourhood. The camp must have been one of the few prosperous places in eastern Wessex during that winter, and offered many possibilities for employment. There would have been all sorts of jobs to be done: digging for defences and latrine pits, care of horses, repair of weapons, smithing, maintenance of huts, and so on. Danish fighting men could turn their hands to most things, but they were the conquerors, so why should they? The long winter nights demanded entertainment, food and ale, harping and minstrelsy, and female companionship. A number of women were probably seized, but some doubtless came of their own free will, and may even have done quite well out of the booty-rich Danes. Those English people engaged in menial tasks could hope for food, even if it was contemptuously tossed to them. The Danish force would not have wanted to clutter up its camp with large numbers of semi-permanent hangers-on, since this would have been too dangerous when the main army was away, so most would have had to live outside the camp itself. Trade has always followed military operations, so it is also very likely that such activity took place, even if on a modest scale and with traders based just outside the camp. Therefore, though we can postulate some breakdown in the normal organization of life among the English inhabitants, it would be rash to assume any substantial break in the occupation of the site of Reading.

This episode was like so many others in history: of very great importance to people at the time, but of no lasting historical effect. No doubt some Reading men took part in the further opposition to the Danes during Alfred's reign, but none of the fighting during the 870s or that of 892–6 involved this immediate neighbourhood. The ordered way of life in Reading, such as it was, was probably resumed as quickly as possible. Those who had fled would have been keen to return rather than remain as refugees. Reading, though strategically placed, was not important enough to become one of the fortified *burhs* which Alfred and his successor established in Wessex, so we have to assume that over the next century or so this settlement resumed its steady but undistinguished existence.

This traumatic period was apparently followed by a century or so of uneventful existence, for there is no further significant mention of Reading until calamity descended once more. The Danish troubles of the late 900s and the early years of the next century had taken on a new character, for they had become a struggle between kings. As political ambition and personal glory gained in importance, all kinds of behaviour became normal, including the most brutal ravaging and destruction. Such actions forced the hand of the English king, who attempted to buy his way out of trouble with vast *gelds*. Unfortunately for England – and for the folk of Reading – the king at this time was the calamitous Ethelræd II, Unræd, the man who would not take advice. Reading folk would have had to pay their share of the hefty sums demanded, but far worse for them was the coming of the Danes.

The Danes passed through this area on various occasions between 1006 and 1013, destroying and looting, 'and ever burning as they went' as the Anglo-Saxon Chronicle puts it. By the end of that time the area must have been a scene of misery and desolation. The Danes burned Reading just before Christmas 1006. Huts could be rebuilt, but for most people it was impossible to replace stores of winter food which had been destroyed or looted. It is possible that a slight recovery had taken place by the time the Danes passed through again in 1009, but in 1010 there can have been little left to ravage. Loyalty to their ineffective king must have been minimal among the English, and there was probably considerable relief when, in 1017, the Danish Cnut (Canute) became king of all England.

Little is known of Reading under the Danish kings, though in the reign of Cnut the manor of Reading seems at one stage to have been held by Tovi, reputedly Cnut's standard-bearer. Legend suggests that the folk of Reading were not renowned for their piety. The story goes

The head of King Cnut on a
silver penny

that Tovi had acquired the holy cross which had been found some
years before at Montacute in Somerset, and wanted to found a
religious house worthy of it. All manner of sites were suggested, but
the efforts of neither oxen nor men could move the cart which was
carrying the cross. Among the sites proposed was his favoured
domicile of Reading, and he tearfully implored Christ to let that be
the place, promising to give the vill and all around to those serving
the holy cross. But it was no good, and it was not until the name of
Waltham was mentioned that cart and oxen set off at speed. So the
future great abbey of Waltham Holy Cross was founded and Reading
was not to have an abbey for nearly another hundred years. But as the
route to Waltham would pass through Reading, the holy cross would
have spent at least a night there.

The Danish dynasty was short-lived, and in 1043 the English line
returned in the shape of Edward, later known as the Confessor.
Reading again became a royal vill, and it was during this reign that it
took its next great step, becoming a borough (*burh*). In the early

fifteenth century it was stated that Reading had been a borough since 'before time that no mind is'; certainly it was one in 1086. Very probably it was one of the many small boroughs created in Edward's reign, and also one of the very small mints created in the early part of that period, for while coinage was firmly controlled by the king, the actual striking of coins was done locally. Many of these small new boroughs did not survive, and a number of the mints coined for only very short periods. All that survive of the output of Reading's mint are three silver pennies, two probably and one possibly dating from the early years of the reign. This suggests a fairly paltry output and closure after the reorganization of more important mints like Wallingford.

It was not its value as a minting centre, therefore, that ensured the survival of Reading as a borough, and on the face of it there was no other obvious reason at all. Trade was, of course, the main justification for a borough, so there must have been some such activity here, but it

King Edward (the Confessor). From the Bayeux Tapestry

King Harold. From the Bayeux Tapestry

was probably at a local level rather than based on manufacturing or international trade.

Of course, the smaller and less significant the borough, the more its inhabitants were involved in local agriculture and the less it would have extricated itself from the local government of hundred and shire. Nevertheless, it was a status greatly to be desired, and there must have been some in this new borough who looked hopefully at the situation in London, Winchester or even Wallingford, the county town, as something to which Reading might aspire. The benefits could include the gaining of the portable wealth that trade engendered, the elimination of rival markets in the vicinity, the exercise of self-government and the development of borough customs, over such matters as inheritance, which could acquire the force of law. Even the poorer members of the community must have appreciated the stress on personal freedom which borough status gave. Taxation is never popular, but the payment of *chepyngavell*, a trading tax, to the king, was a clear indication that some status had been acquired, and at least the first step had been taken in gaining independence from the county authorities.

Who played what part in the acquisition of borough status for this vill we do not know, but there must have been considerable local satisfaction, and visions stretching into the future of steadily developing prosperity and self-government under a native monarchy. Few in the country could have foreseen the happenings of 1066, which marked the end of the English dynasty and the imposition of alien rule (for that, no matter what William of Normandy claimed about being 'right heir', was what happened). It is doubtful whether any men from Reading fought at distant Stamford Bridge, but it is quite possible that men from this locality were at the Battle of Hastings. And a trading community was well placed to hear the spate of news and rumours which must have preceded the actual appearance of William's army on its way to crossing the Thames at Wallingford.

There is no evidence that Reading was badly damaged: in fact, it was soon able to fund an increased payment to the crown. But this does not mean that individuals did not suffer during this tough and brutal episode. As William moved in a curve around London, he established castles to protect his flank to the west, and Reading was

Soldiers of the English army fighting on foot against the Norman cavalry at the Battle of Hastings. From the Bayeux Tapestry

William the Conqueror. From the Bayeux Tapestry

on a main route. The history of many towns was affected by the foundations of a castle within their bounds, but Reading was apparently too insignificant to need a castle to keep it under control, and the names of Castle Street and Castle Hill point towards a site then outside the town. Sites suggested have included the old gaol in Castle Street and the mound in Prospect Park. Any such building would have only been a temporary structure to serve a temporary purpose, and nothing more is known of it. Nor have any archaeological traces been identified of what must have been a wooden palisade on an earth mound. And though trade notoriously follows the flag, Reading was not significant enough at this time to attract the settlement of foreign merchants.

It is twenty years after the Norman Conquest that we have in Domesday Book the first real, though tantalizingly brief, glimpse of what was essentially late Saxon Reading. It was described as a borough and 59 properties were mentioned. About half of these (28) were plots probably containing more than one dwelling, and these larger or better-off holdings paid 100s. a year to the king for all dues; they had previously paid £4 3s. Of the remainder there were 29

The entry in Domesday Book for the land in Reading held by the king. It translates:

Reading. King Edward held it. Then and now it answered for 43 hides. Land for 40 ploughs. In lordship 1; 55 villagers and 30 smallholders with 55 ploughs. 4 mills at 55 shillings; 3 fisheries at 14 shillings and 6 pence; meadow, 150 acres; woodland at 100 pigs; from the pasture 16 shillings and 6 pence. Value before 1066 and later £40; now £48.

In the Borough of Reading the King has 28 properties which pay £4 3 shillings for all customary dues; however their holders pay 100 shillings. Henry of Ferrers has 1 property and half a virgate of land, in which are 3 acres of meadow. Value 6 shillings. Godric, the Sheriff, held this land for hospitality purposes; therefore Henry holds it. Reinbald, son of Bishop Peter, held 1 property there which he transferred to his manor of Earley. Now it is in the King's hands; value 16 pence.

[Facsimile of a medieval Latin manuscript entry from the Domesday Book]

Battle Abbey was given land in Reading by William. The Domesday Book entry translates:

> The Abbot holds a church in Reading himself with 8 hides which belong to it. Abbess Leofeva held it from King Edward. Then it answered for 8 hides; now for 3 hides. Land for 7 ploughs. In lordship 1; 9 villagers and 8 smallholders with 5 ploughs. 2 mills at 40 shillings; 2 and a half fisheries at 5 shillings. In Reading, 29 dwellings at 28 shillings and 8 pence; meadow, 12 acres; woodland at 5 pigs; from the church £3. Value before 1066 £9; Later £8; now £11.

The church estate lay in the manor of Reading. The part concerning the Borough is 'In Reding, 29 dwellings at 28 shillings and 8 pence . . .'

smaller properties, possibly individual houses, and the king had granted the annual income of 28s. 8d. from these to his newly founded abbey of St Martin of Battle, built on the site of his victory near Hastings. One of the two remaining houses, a modest dwelling, had been held by Reinbald, son of bishop Peter, but was now in the king's hands. The other seems to have been the most imposing in the borough. It had previously been held by the sheriff for entertaining official guests, and was now held by Henry de Ferrers for the same purpose. The house had several acres of land attached to it, including three acres of meadow, probably to provide for the guests. As it stood in a fair-sized estate it would certainly have been set apart from the other dwellings, probably on or near the later abbey site, and traces of late-Saxon cultivation have been identified on the north side of Holy Brook.

Reading's church served much more than the town. Although not named in Domesday Book, it was certainly St Mary's, and it was well off, for it rendered £3 a year to the Abbot of Battle. That abbot's estate, the later manor of Battle, had been held under Edward the Confessor by Abbess Leveva. It has been suggested that she was the last abbess of a defunct nunnery here, possibly founded in 979. Various guesses have been made about its location, but it was probably situated in the region of the latter abbey, for excavation in a small area at the east end of the abbey church showed flint-in-mortar foundations underlying those of the abbey.

In addition to these buildings, possibly one or two of the Domesday mills along the Kennet were situated in the town area. So how many inhabitants did Reading have at this time? Any answer must be very speculative, but the total would perhaps be around five hundred or a little higher. This would make Reading much smaller than the other Berkshire borough, Wallingford, but large enough for a recognizable and self-governing community.

Few other traces of Saxon Reading remain. The name, as we have seen, is Saxon, as are many of the names of places close by – Coley, Earley, Whitley, Fobney and Caversham, for example. Many of the field-names of the manor of Reading were also Saxon. Within the town most names have changed with the centuries or have been newly coined as the town has expanded. Nevertheless a few still recall this remote past: Minster Street, which led to the minster church; Vastern Road, which recalls the vasterns, derived from the Old English word for a stronghold, and possibly referring to the Danish camp; Cadel, the owner of a grove, survived in *Cadelesgroue*, now Katesgrove; Portmanbrook, a name current well into the nineteenth century, remembers the inhabitants of the *port*, Anglo-Saxon for trading-place; Tothill, the name for the north end of Minster Street until well into the Middle Ages, is *tot-hyll*, 'lookout hill', marking the time when Reading clustered around St Mary's and the Old Market, with no Broad Street or buildings impeding the view, and New Street and New Market unthought of; Forbury is the area in front of the town; it is also possible that the Middle English names of Mill Lane and High Bridge are later forms of the Saxon. These traces are few, but Reading nevertheless has its roots in Saxon times: in the settlement itself, in its very name, and in the first steps in the development of the borough of Reading.

2

Reading Abbey and the Medieval Town

BRIAN KEMP

This chapter is concerned with Reading in the Middle Ages, taking the story on from early Norman times into the sixteenth century. The single most important factor in the history of Reading in this period was the existence of Reading Abbey, founded by Henry I in 1121 and dissolved by Henry VIII in 1539.

The establishment of Reading Abbey undoubtedly had a very considerable effect, both on the physical appearance and development of the town, and on its economic and constitutional development. However, we must be careful not to exaggerate this, since the little town of Reading, as it is revealed in the Domesday Book of 1086, already possessed many geographical and other advantages which would no doubt have led to its economic growth and prosperity, whether the abbey was there or not. It was a royal vill, with all the potential benefits which that entailed, and its geographical position favoured economic advance; it was situated at the crossing of major land routes, north-south and west-east, and, although built on the banks of the River Kennet, a valuable asset in itself, it was also so close to the Thames that it could not fail to benefit from the access to London by river which the junction of the Kennet with the Thames afforded. Moreover, the abbey's influence on the town was felt mainly and most profoundly during the first 150–200 years after the monks arrived: that is, down to the early fourteenth century, by which time

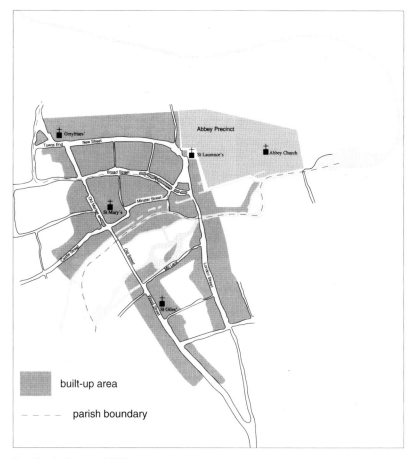

Reading in the later Middle Ages

the town's growing prosperity had acquired a momentum which could henceforth be only marginally affected by the abbey.

It would be wrong, therefore, to claim that Reading Abbey alone enabled or caused the Domesday *burgus* of Reading to transform itself into the most prosperous town of Berkshire in the later Middle Ages. But what the abbey did was to provide a powerful boost to the town's economic growth, to act as a catalyst to the inherent advantages of the town's situation, and to bring, through its own privileges and rights, benefits which the townspeople could enjoy and exploit. This is not the place to enter into a detailed history of the abbey, but in order to give some idea of its impact on the development of the town, it is necessary to look at certain key facts.

The first and probably the most important point to be made is that Reading Abbey was a royal abbey, founded by a king and remaining under royal patronage until the Dissolution. The founder, Henry I, was determined to begin a new monastery which would not only proclaim his devotion to Holy Mother Church, but would also receive his body for burial after death: in other words, he intended it to be a royal mausoleum. For this new house the king chose Cluniac monks, belonging to a reformed and splendid type of Black Benedictine monasticism centred on the great abbey of Cluny in Burgundy. In response to the king's request to Abbot Pons, eight monks from Cluny were sent to England, where they were joined by several others from the Cluniac priory of St Pancras at Lewes. The whole party arrived in Reading on 18 June 1121 to inaugurate monastic life in the monastery newly founded by the king. For nearly two years the house was a priory, not yet an abbey, the monks living under the direction of Prior Peter, who had been among the original eight monks from Cluny. But on 15 April 1123 the first abbot was appointed, Hugh of Amiens, formerly Prior of Lewes, and Prior Peter returned to Cluny. It seems that until the arrival of the first abbot the infant house at Reading was under some sort of control from Cluny, but when it became an abbey it was freed from all subjection to Cluny or any other Cluniac house. Reading was thus an abbey following the Cluniac observance but juridically independent; this was a most unusual circumstance, but one which suited the founder's desires admirably.

To enhance the setting of his final resting-place, Henry I built, or at least began the building of, a magnificent church and a group of

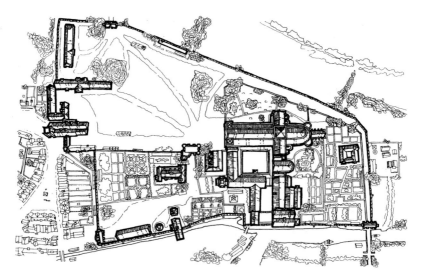

The layout of the thirty acres of the abbey within the perimeter wall in the sixteenth century. From a conjectural reconstruction model

monastic buildings set in a precinct of about thirty acres on the eastern edge of the little town of Reading. The abbey church itself took quite a time to build, and work on it was interrupted during the troubles of Stephen's reign, but it was far enough advanced by April 1164 for its solemn dedication by Archbishop Thomas Becket to take place. It was a lofty cruciform building of impressive size and appearance, with a massive central tower rising over the crossing. It had an aisled nave and an aisled apsidal choir with chapels radiating off, and north and south transepts with projecting eastern chapels. Apart from the rebuilding of the eastern chapel of the choir in the early fourteenth century to make a fine new Lady Chapel, no major alterations were made to the original plan. The full length of the church was 450 feet, its width 95 feet, and the width across the transepts 200 feet; the overall area was something like that of the present Salisbury Cathedral.

To the south of the church were the monastic buildings, ranged around a quadrangular cloister in typical Benedictine fashion. Projecting south from the south transept were the chapter house and dormitory range with the *domus necessaria*; along the south side of the cloister was the refectory; and along the west side the cellarer's range. Most of the walls were very sturdy and thick, constructed of flint in mortar and faced with fine dressed stone, mostly from the king's ducal quarries in Normandy. All in all the gleaming walls of the great abbey rising alongside the town symbolized the wealth, importance and authority of the abbot and convent.

To sustain the splendour of the Cluniac liturgy and provide for the physical and spiritual welfare of the monks, Henry richly endowed the abbey with lands, churches and privileges. When augmented by gifts from his contemporaries and from others in subsequent reigns, these were to result in Reading Abbey becoming one of the richest and most powerful religious houses in England. Among Henry's own grants was that of the manor and town of Reading; this meant that

The abbey church viewed from the north-west. A conjectural view

now the abbot and the monks, rather than the king, were lords of the town. We shall need to return to this point later.

According to Henry's scheme, as well as being a centre of monastic excellence and spiritual fervour, the abbey was also to dispense hospitality to travellers and pilgrims, as well as relief to the poor. In other words, it was not to be an exclusive closed house, but one active in charitable work, and we know from the testimony of William of Malmesbury, a monk of Malmesbury Abbey in Wiltshire, that the Reading monks quickly acquired a fine reputation for unstinted generosity. Moreover, the abbey founded two hospitals within the precinct during the twelfth century: Abbot Anscher's for lepers (St Mary Magdalene) in 1130–5, and Abbot Hugh II's for the poor and pilgrims (St John the Baptist, at the Abbey Gate) in the early 1190s.

Furthermore, in pursuance of Henry I's intentions, the abbey served as a mausoleum, not only for the king but also for other members of his family down to the middle of Henry II's reign: Henry I was buried in the abbey church in January 1136; his second queen and widow Adeliza in 1151; William, the young son of Henry II, in 1156; and Reginald, Earl of Cornwall and natural son of Henry I, in 1175. Thereafter Fontevrault and, later, Westminster took over the role of royal mausoleum, but as late as 1232 and 1234 the infant son and daughter of Richard, Earl of Cornwall and Henry III's brother, were buried at Reading.

Since it had been founded by a king, Reading Abbey, like all royal foundations, continued under the patronage of all subsequent English kings until its dissolution. This meant not only that the king was obliged to ensure the maintenance of its status and rights (though this was not always carried out to the monks' full satisfaction), but also that there rested on the abbey the obligation of entertaining and accommodating the king when he chose to visit Reading. As a consequence, medieval kings frequently stayed in the abbey, particularly in the twelfth and thirteenth centuries, sometimes for several days or even weeks. At these times the monks had to provide lodging for the king and members of his family, and also for his senior courtiers and ministers. On some of these occasions events notable in the history of the realm at large took place in the abbey, such as the marriage of Edward III's son, John of Gaunt, to Blanche of Lancaster in 1359, and the public celebration of Edward IV's marriage in 1464. Reading Abbey's close connection with the Crown and the frequent lodging of royalty in the abbey derived, as we have seen, from the fact that it was founded by a king, but the geographical position of Reading and the facilities available at the abbey also meant that it received visits from other important people and was chosen for the holding of various lay and ecclesiastical assemblies from time to time, most notably Parliament on three occasions in the fifteenth century.

There is also the fact of Reading Abbey's religious and artistic importance, which drew people to Reading as pilgrims, visitors or searchers after spiritual guidance. This aspect was particularly important in the twelfth century, when monasteries were still the main

A page from a twelfth-century book from Reading Abbey with the manuscript of Paschasius Radbertus's '*Liber de Benedictionibus Patriarchum*' ('Book on the Blessings of the Patriarchs'), the only known copy of this work

A carved but broken Caen stone capital of *c.* 1125 from Reading Abbey, showing the earliest representation of the Coronation of the Virgin. Christ on the right holds a book in one hand and places a crown on the Virgin's head with the other

powerhouses of the Church, and especially so for the small town of Reading, which was beginning to grow in the early years of the abbey's existence. Like other monasteries, Reading maintained a constant round of prayer and intercession to God. The monks, following the rule of St Benedict, daily attended the night office and the seven canonical day offices, as well as the high mass and other services, in addition to their private study and devotions. But there was also at Reading in the twelfth century a special devotion to the Blessed Virgin Mary. The abbey had been founded in honour of St Mary and St John the Evangelist, and on its first common seal the Virgin was depicted seated with the Christ-child on her lap. Moreover, the first abbot was influential in the introduction of the cult of the Immaculate Conception, making arrangements for the celebration of this novel feast at Reading. It is no coincidence that the earliest surviving depiction of the Coronation of the Virgin in European art appears on one of the carved capitals from the abbey, now in the Reading Museum and Art Gallery. The monks also possessed relics of the Virgin Mary, including a hair (though even the monks were uncertain about this), and parts of her robe, girdle and sepulchre.

These were merely a few among the abbey's large and varied collection of relics, which numbered well over two hundred by the end of the twelfth century. Relics of the saints were of the greatest importance at this time in popular religious devotion, not only locally but further afield as well, and they inevitably added to the flow of pilgrims to the abbey. A surviving list of Reading Abbey's relics made in the 1190s gives 237 different pieces, but adds that there were 'also many other relics, whose labels are missing'. The list is arranged in categories: relics of the Cross and our Lord (28), of the Virgin Mary (6), Patriarchs and Prophets (18), Apostles (12), Martyrs (73), Confessors (51), and Holy Virgins (49).

By far the most important relic was the Hand of St James, brought from Germany in 1126 by Henry I's daughter, the Empress Matilda, and deposited by the king in Reading Abbey a few years later. Although lost from the abbey in Stephen's reign, it was returned in 1155 at Henry II's command and remained there afterwards until the Dissolution. A major cult of St James grew up at Reading in the second half of the twelfth century, based on the Hand, and assisted by episcopal grants of indulgence for his feast-day (25 July) and by papal approval. Pilgrims began to flock to Reading and miracles were performed by the Hand – mostly healing miracles. St James became so prominent in the abbey's identity that he was soon added to its tutelary saints, and his emblem, a scallop shell, began to appear on the abbey's seals in the early thirteenth century. Later it was to form its coat of arms: three golden scallops on a blue field.

We know something about the kind of miracles worked by the Hand from a manuscript of around 1200, which describes twenty-

Left: A thirteenth-century counterseal of the abbey, showing the hand of St James between two scallops. *Above*: An early fourteenth-century 'taxation' seal, showing the earliest known representations of the abbey's coat of arms

eight miracles, and we also know about the reliquary for the Hand. Its original reliquary was replaced by a new one between 1163 and 1187, but this was taken by Richard I in 1189 and replaced by a third one out of Count John's generous grant of one mark of gold per year. This gift is but one example of John's close relations with Reading Abbey, both before and after be became king. He also gave another major apostolic relic to the monks in 1205: the Head of St Philip (from Constantinople). We know from a later source that with it he gave a rich reliquary to contain it: 'a golden casket enriched with precious stones'. This sort of reference is the only clue we now have about the enormous wealth of the abbey in gold and silver vessels, for none has actually survived.

Similarly, very little has survived of the rich architecture of the abbey, with the very important exception of the splendid series of carved capitals and other stones from the twelfth-century cloister, which are now in Reading Museum. These give a hint of the richness of carved detail that once abounded throughout the abbey. This is also evident in a beautiful stone head of a bishop or episcopal saint, dating from the thirteenth century, which has recently come to light.

A fragment of the abbey's legacy in music has, happily, come down to us. In addition to some elaborate polyphonic liturgical pieces from the thirteenth and fourteenth centuries, we have the famous *Sumer is icumen in*. Known as the Reading Round, this is the earliest surviving round for several voices and dates from the middle of the thirteenth century.

A number of encaustic floor tiles have been discovered, some of very high quality. We also know of at least two statues formerly present in the abbey, which depicted the Christ-child and the Virgin. The artistic

A carved limestone captial of *c.* 1125 from the abbey cloisters showing seated winged figures

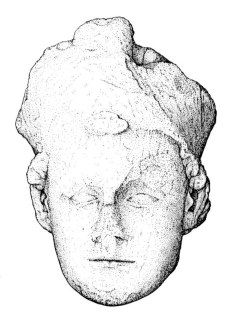

A thirteenth-century head of a mitred saint or bishop from a life-size limestone standing statue

excellence aspired to by the monks is also evident in the beautiful series of abbey seals, especially the superb second common seal made in 1328, although where their matrices were made is unknown.

No stained glass, rich textiles, vestments or precious vessels have survived, but from what we have and all that we know, we can, with a leap of the imagination, gain a hazy idea of the splendour in which the monastic round was carried on at Reading in the Middle Ages.

As befitted the head of so noble an abbey, the abbot was an important figure in the locality and in the realm as a whole. In 1191 the abbot received from the pope the right to wear episcopal vestments, including the mitre. From this date Reading is regarded as a 'mitred' abbey. From the time when parliaments were first held, in Henry III's reign, the abbot of Reading was regularly summoned to attend as a lord spiritual of the realm: Reading in the Middle Ages was thus one of the so-called 'parliamentary' abbeys.

The earliest recorded four-part round in Britain, *Summer is icumen in*. From a thirteenth-century manuscript from Reading Abbey (Harley MS 978 f.11b)

Encaustic tiles from the thirteenth-century cloister walkways of Reading Abbey

We have gone into this degree of detail about Reading Abbey in order to emphasize the kind of institution which was established by Henry I on the edge of the little town of Reading, over which it exercised lordship. What effects did this great abbey have on the town?

Firstly, there was an impact on its physical development. The centre of gravity of the town moved under the abbey's influence from its old location in the Butts area eastward towards the abbey; a new market was established on the western side of the abbey precinct wall;

The seal of Abbot Nicholas of Whaplode (1305–28), showing the standing figure of the abbot in a niche flanked by emblems of St James

The obverse of the abbey's second common seal (1328), showing the Virgin and Child between St James and St John the Evangelist

Part of an early sixteenth-century manuscript, showing the Abbot of Reading in procession to Parliament (Ashmole Rolls 45)

and new streets were laid out in the vicinity of the abbey. The most important of these was New Street (now Friar Street), which extended west of the Main or Compter Gate of the abbey, to the north of the earlier settlement in Reading. A new parish and parish church also appeared, St Laurence's. The church of St Laurence began life as a chapel alongside the Main Gate, a standard feature of all large abbeys, in order to provide an oratory for pilgrims arriving at the abbey before they proceeded to the abbey church itself. St Laurence's, which was being called a church by the beginning of the thirteenth century, thus owed its existence entirely to the abbey. For its parish it was assigned the newly developed area around what is now Friar Street and the land to the north and west.

The economic benefits which the abbey brought to the town were also considerable, though they were not the sole factor in Reading's economic growth in the Middle Ages. The abbey was a major employer of labour and services in the town and its hinterland. The number of monks in the abbey varied from period to period, but if we think of something like a hundred monks in its heyday, we shall probably not be far wrong. But there would also have been at least as many lay servants in the monastery, recruited from the town or the abbey's estates. In addition to these, many other servants would have been employed who did not live in the monastery but in the town or nearby. All these normal needs of the abbey would, of course, be greatly amplified when the king or another important visitor came to visit or stay at the abbey with his entourage, or when great gatherings of church councils and parliaments met there.

The enormous amount of business generated by the abbey for the catering and supply trades in the town can only be guessed at, but that it was a considerable boost to the town's economic life cannot be doubted. The practitioners of some trades were so numerous that from

St Mary's church, the Butts, Reading. From an engraving of 1801

quite early times craft guilds for them came into being, the earliest being those of the vintners and the drapers, which were in existence by the middle of the thirteenth century. By the early fourteenth century at the latest, certain parts of the town were set aside for particular kinds of tradesmen – butchers, fishmongers, shoemakers, lorimers, drapers and so on – and the surnames of Reading folk in the later Middle Ages reveal a whole host of other trading activities.

In addition to all this and the weekly markets, the abbey obtained the right to hold annual fairs at Reading. These brought profit to the monks as lords of Reading, and also, of course, gave a further stimulus to the town's prosperity. The first was St Laurence's Fair, granted by the founder of the abbey, to be held on the feast day itself (10 August) and on the three days following. The next was St James's Fair, granted by Henry II possibly in 1164, again for the feast day (25 July) and the three days following. The last was the Fair of St Philip and St James the Less, granted by King John in 1205, to be held on the vigil and feast day (1 May) and the two days following.

St Laurence's Fair fell out of use in the early fourteenth century. It is interesting to note that the other two fairs were definitely granted in association with important relics housed in the abbey. It seems likely, therefore, that St Laurence's Fair was also related to relics in the abbey. If this was so, it would mean that the pieces of the body and blood of St Laurence, with coals, which appear in the late twelfth-century relic list, were already in the monks' possession in Henry I's time and were then regarded as particularly important, perhaps even given by the king himself. This may also explain the dedication of the new chapel at the Main Gate to St Laurence. Be that as it may, it is clear that the times of major fairs in Reading were chiefly determined by the relics held in the abbey. These were equally, of course, times when pilgrims and others would flock to the abbey to take advantage of its indulgences, and hence also boost the catering and trading activities of the town. Townspeople also benefited from the abbey's privileges in trading further afield, especially in other markets and

St Laurence's church. From an
engraving of 1804

fairs, since both the founder and later kings confirmed the rights of
the abbey and all its men to freedom from tolls and other customs
payments throughout England.

But there was another side to the economic benefit which the town
derived from having the abbey on its doorstep. This concerned the
abbey's lordship of the town and the government of its affairs. Before
the foundation of the abbey the town's lord was the king, an absent
figure who did not take a close interest in its affairs. With the arrival
of the monks, however, the town passed under the lordship of an
immediately resident, powerful and undying institution which was
keen to preserve its rights and authority in the town: the abbot and
convent. At first there appears to have been no problem in this
respect, but the town grew in prosperity and self-confidence, and by
the end of the thirteenth century was sending its own representatives
to Parliament. In these circumstances the abbey's lordship became

49

irksome and was even the cause of open conflict and violence in the mid-thirteenth century. Nevertheless, although difficulties occurred on and off until the abbey's dissolution, there was, on the whole, a marked lack of major insurrection or rioting by the townspeople against the abbey, such as happened, for example, at St Albans, Abingdon, Bury St Edmunds and elsewhere.

When they did arise, the disputes were generally conducted in a civilized manner through the courts of law, no doubt because both the abbey and the town recognized the mutual benefit derived from their close physical and constitutional relationship. The conflict which arose in the thirteenth century was essentially between the abbot and his bailiffs, who ran the town on his behalf, and the increasingly important gild (the gild merchant) which represented the leading townsmen. The latter complained on this occasion about various alleged oppressions by the abbey, which had undermined their ancient liberties. By 1253 the burgesses were even 'lying in wait day and night for the abbot's bailiffs' and 'assaulting them in the execution of their office'. Although the king's court investigated the matter and the king ordered the maintenance of the abbey's authority, the burgesses succeeded in obtaining from the king a charter conferring extensive privileges throughout England to 'the burgesses of Reading who belong to the Gild Merchant of Reading'.

This was not the end of the matter, however, for in 1254 the dispute was brought before the court of King's Bench (*coram rege*) for settlement. On this occasion the stewards of the gild, Henry Wille and Daniel Wolvesey, and the burgesses complained against the abbot on four points: he had forced them to plead elsewhere than in their common gildhall; he had removed from them their gild merchant; he had moved the market from its ancient site; and he was exacting customs and services to which he had no right.

A settlement was reached and embodied in a type of legal document known as a final concord. In it the abbot granted that the corn market should be restored to its previous site, all other types of merchandise being sold equally in their old places; the burgesses should have their gildhall with twelve appurtenant messuages and Portmanbrook meadow for half a mark per annum instead of 1d. as before; and they should have their gild merchant as before. In return the burgesses conceded that the abbot had the right to choose one of the gildsmen to be warden (*custos*) of the gild on an annual basis; that he was to receive entry fines from new gildsmen, and 5d. per annum as *Chepinggavel* from each gild-merchant burgess; that the abbot might tallage (tax) Reading town when the king tallaged his demesne; and that the abbot or his bailiffs might hold pleas in the gildhall, the key of which was normally to remain with the warden.

This settlement, which appears basically to have restored the *status quo* before recent changes brought about by the abbot, remained in force in essentials thereafter, though modified in detail from the mid-fourteenth century onwards. Moreover the title of warden of the gild gradually gave way to that of Mayor of Reading by the end of the thirteenth century, although this was not recognized by the abbey, which continued to refer to the warden of the gild.

Various sources of irritation arose in the later Middle Ages. In the mid-fourteenth century trouble occurred over the election of constables in the town, and in the mid-fifteenth there was a dispute over a mace for the mayor. It appears that Henry VI granted the warden of the gild the right to have a mace; later, on learning that this was contrary to the abbey's liberties, he withdrew the right. In a letter to the warden he stated that the only symbols of authority to be borne in the town were to be the two tipped staves of the abbot's bailiffs. However, the status and importance of the gild merchant were growing all the time, and in 1487 Henry VII granted an important gild charter recognizing the title of 'Mayor and burgesses of Reading', which somewhat curtailed the abbot's rights over the burgesses. A few years later, around 1500, a rather complicated dispute arose over a number of very specific matters, in the course of which the townsmen advanced the argument that the gild merchant was a corporate body.

Hugh Faringdon, the last
Abbot of Reading. From
a stained-glass window
originally in the country
lodging of the Abbot of
Reading at Bere Court,
near Reading

Even so, the settlement of the dispute in 1507 basically left the
abbot's lordship of the town intact, but with the significant proviso
that now the abbot was to choose the new mayor from three
burgesses proposed by the corporate body of mayor and burgesses.
And so the situation remained until the dissolution of the abbey.

Reading Abbey was dissolved in 1539 as part of the sweeping
religious changes of Henry VIII's reign. In the early 1530s Parliament
swept away papal authority over the English Church and substituted
the authority of the king. In addition, for financial and allegedly
religious reasons, the government also planned to dissolve all the
monasteries. The smaller houses were dissolved *en bloc* in 1536, but
the larger ones, including Reading, were to be induced to surrender
voluntarily to the Crown in the next few years. Most did so, but
Abbot Hugh Cooke Faringdon of Reading refused. Though
previously on good terms with Henry VIII and officiating at the
obsequies of Queen Jane (Seymour) in 1537, the abbot found himself

charged with treason in 1539. He was probably in the Tower of London by September 1539, and by 19 September the town authorities in Reading regarded the abbot as having been deprived and the abbey as already suppressed.

What we do know is that the abbot was returned to Reading for his trial, which took place before a commission of oyer and terminer on 13 November 1539. He was duly convicted of treason for denying the royal supremacy over the English Church, and was executed the following day, 14 November. The outcome was, however, a foregone conclusion, to judge from a note in the hand of Thomas Cromwell, Henry VIII's vicegerent in spirituals, which reads:

> The abbot of Reading to be sent down to be tried and executed at Reading with his accomplices . . . counsellors to give evidence against the abbot of Reading, Mr Hynde and the king's attorney . . . See that the evidence be well sorted and the indictments well drawn.

The chapter house. Pen, ink and water-colour by S.H. Grimm (1733–94)

East view of the abbey ruins. From an engraving by Charles Tomkins of 1791

The ruins of the abbey's chapter house from the south in 1984, before conservation

The details of the abbot's indictment were discovered in the Public Record Office in the 1950s. It is clear that the evidence was all hearsay. For example, it was reported that, in 1536, the abbot had said,

> The king is not supreme head of the Church of England and I trust to see the Pope bear as great a rule in England as ever he did shortly and I will say mass once every week for him.

This sort of thing was enough to condemn him. Following the abbot's execution, the monks were dispersed, and the abbey and all its possessions escheated to the Crown and became Crown property. Thus in this sad but also heroic way the abbey as a corporate institution disappeared, and a long formative chapter in the history of Reading came to an end.

3

Reading in the Sixteenth and Seventeenth Centuries

JOAN DILS

In St Laurence's church there is a small monumental brass, which is all that remains of the imposing grey marble tomb of Edward Butler, five times Mayor of the Borough of Reading, who died in 1584. His long life of seventy-two years spanned some of the greatest changes in the history of the town, which occurred in the years following the dissolution of the abbey. The last abbot, Hugh Faringdon, was executed in 1539, when Butler was already a grown man of twenty-seven.

With the Dissolution, for the first time in four hundred years Reading again became a royal borough, administered by the king's steward. The understeward was a local man, Thomas Vachell: he was one of the Members of Parliament for the borough and had assisted with the Dissolution from which he made a substantial profit. Vachell and his family acquired several of the abbey's properties in the town, and it was to his house that its valuable plate, vestments and jewels were taken to await secure transport to London. There they would add more wealth to the royal coffers.

The actual destruction of the abbey buildings came a few years later. After the death of Henry VIII, and during the early years of the reign of his young son Edward, the country was ruled by Edward Seymour, Duke of Somerset and uncle of the king. It is possible that he gave his name to Duke Street; certainly he was given the lordship of Reading as one of the many acquisitions which made him extremely wealthy. During 1549 much of what was valuable in the abbey, from the lead on the roof to the wood of the monks' stalls, was either sent to London for the duke or sold. St Mary's church was repaired with seventy cart loads of materials from the site, and many local houses must have acquired woodwork or tiles from the same source. Later, in the Charter granted by Elizabeth I, Reading was given two hundred loads of 'ragged or free stones' from the monastery and the timber and tiles from other abbey buildings to repair the 'ruinous' bridges of the town.

By the time Edward Butler died only a few traces of the once great monastery remained to serve as stables and accommodation during royal visits. The physical impact on the appearance of the town must have been enormous; one can only guess at the psychological effect on Edward Butler and the other citizens.

The administrative impact was slower in coming but altogether more significant. In 1542, and more importantly in 1560, the borough of Reading was given royal charters increasing its size, power and wealth. The town extended its boundaries to the whole manor of Reading, and became a free corporate borough with a council made up of nine capital burgesses and twelve secondary burgesses named in the charter of 1560. This was no democracy: the burgesses had the power to choose their successors. Every year from among their ranks they appointed the borough officials, such as the cofferers who administered the finances, and elected a mayor. The first holder of this office under the new regime of 1560 was Edward Butler.

The corporation took over the repair of the nineteen bridges in the town and the running of the school – duties very inadequately performed by the Crown in the twenty or so years since the end of the abbey. In return, the corporation was given nearly three hundred former monastic possessions in the town. These included houses, inns, barns and meadows, whose rents were to provide much of the corporation's income. The rest came mostly from the tolls on produce coming to market, fees paid to use the wharves on the

A rubbing from part of the remains of the brass of Edward Butler in St Laurence's church. Butler was originally shown with Alice, his wife of forty-two years, and his daughters, Alice, Mary and Elizabeth

Kennet and the fines levied in the courts. Most of the property in Reading not owned by the borough had been purchased in 1545 by William Grey, 'the King's Servant', for £2,133 3s. Grey bought the manor of Bulmershe in the same year and the manor and town lands eventually became the property of the Blagraves through Grey's marriage to Agnes, who was a widow with a son, John Blagrave. The names of Blagrave and Vachell, two families whose fortunes were so closely linked with the fall of the abbey, are commemorated in the streets of modern Reading.

So too is the name of the other institution which disappeared almost at the same time as the abbey: Greyfriars. This was a Franciscan priory which gave its name to Friar Street. It was dissolved in 1538 and despoiled of its plate, 'such as it ys', wrote Dr London, the commissioner in charge of the dissolution. In his letter to his master, Thomas Cromwell, he added that it was then further

Borough charters were very important documents, enshrining the privileges of the town. As such they were often embellished with elaborate initial letters. This charter, granted to Reading in 1638 by Charles I, bears his portrait in the first letter. It gave the borough rights in addition to those granted in 1560

An early nineteenth-century engraving of the monument in St Laurence's church to John Blagrave of Southcote, grandson of Agnes Grey. Blagrave holds a globe and quadrant, which signify his fame as a mathematician. He died in 1611

denuded by the 'poor people', who 'fell to stealing so fast in every corner of the house that I have been fain to tarry a whole week here to set everything in due order'. The priory church was still serviceable, however, and by 1543 it became the new town hall where council meetings were held. It replaced the old gild (yield) hall near the Kennet where, it was claimed, the noise of the women at 'the common washing place' beating their clothes in the stream made it impossible for the councillors to hear themselves speak. A few years later the councillors again moved their meeting-place, this time to the upper floor of the hospitium or guest house of the former abbey. The ground floor housed the grammar school, and one wonders whether it was any quieter than the council's original home near the Kennet. Once the councillors had departed, part of the former Greyfriars was used, certainly by 1578, as a hospital and later as a house of correction for those poor who refused to work.

The years immediately following the Dissolution were probably difficult ones in Reading, either despite or because of the town's new independence from the abbey. According to the tax receipts of the lay subsidy granted by Parliament for King Henry's wars in France, the borough had been the tenth richest provincial town in England in the 1520s, the last decade before the great changes in the borough's fortunes. In two years Berkshire contributed £3,100, and Reading paid over £420 of this. Moreover, the tax was not levied on the clergy, so the great wealth of the abbey was not assessed. But there are hints in the records that in the 1540s there were difficulties: the mayor's allowance was cut by twenty per cent in 1546, and even so the corporation had to borrow £6 from the churchwardens of St Laurence's parish. This indicates a serious decline in the town's income, which did not yet include the profits on markets or fairs, since these were still going to the Crown. In 1543–4, and far more seriously in 1558–9, there were two epidemics in the borough, the first probably plague and the second almost certainly influenza. The large number of dead included many mature men and women, thus depriving Reading of its wealth producers. This, combined with the loss of income now that visitors no longer came to the abbey, and a downturn in the cloth industry, did not make the first years of the new regime easy ones.

Most significant of all were the changes in religious practice and belief imposed by successive rulers from Henry VIII to Elizabeth I. Henry's changes were mainly confined to Church government, but in the reign of his son, Edward VI, the official religion of England became at first a moderate and then a more extreme form of Protestantism. Reading parishioners would have noticed – perhaps with enthusiasm, perhaps with dismay – the disappearance from their three parish churches of the familiar statues, the rood-screens with their crucifixes, the lights and the vestments. In their place arrived the whitewashed walls adorned only with scriptural texts, services in English, the all-important sermon and the metric psalms.

The fortunate survival of the accounts of the sales and purchases made in this period by the churchwardens of the parishes of St Giles and St Laurence show in graphic detail how the interiors of the churches were transformed. At St Giles they paid for the replacement of the stone altar with a wooden table, purchased an English Bible and Book of Common Prayer, and whitewashed over the painted saints on the church walls. To 'white-lime' St Laurence's church took two men twenty-three days and cost the churchwardens 17s. 3d. Some of the cost would have been met by the sale of the side altars: William Grey paid 10s. 8d. for the marble Trinity altar, while other local men paid lesser sums for those dedicated to St Thomas, St Clement and St John. In 1554 what may have been the first signs of a change in the beliefs of the ordinary people appeared. When Thomas Kent of Southcote in St Mary's parish made his will, he did not, as was traditional, include a request for the intercession of the Virgin Mary and the saints to secure his hope of salvation. Instead he entrusted his soul to God, 'that through and by the merits of Christ his passion it shall be saved'.

But by 1554 the Catholic Mary Tudor was queen, and the churchwardens were beginning to put back their altars, and buy back or bring out of hiding the vestments and Latin mass books. In 1559 they had to remove them all over again when Elizabeth reversed the policies of her sister, and by the Acts of Uniformity and Supremacy brought back the reformed religion of her brother Edward and the royal supremacy of her father, Henry VIII.

No one, least of all the people of Reading, was to know that this settlement would be the one which would last. They had seen their church plate (apart from the few vessels needed for the simpler reformed services) confiscated by the Crown, although, fortunately, the churchwardens of St Laurence's had prudently sold some before the king's officials could seize them, and used the proceeds to repair the roads. People had seen the disappearance of their old festivals and the associated celebrations: Hocktide, and the plays of Robin Hood and St George. Gone too were parish gilds, which provided the comfortable reassurance of prayers for the dead. How long was it before the people accepted the new ideas and became convinced Protestants?

By the 1570s most people were writing 'Protestant' wills like Thomas Kent, and by the 1580s everyone was: perhaps by then they had come to believe the new Creed. When Edward Butler wrote his will in 1584, he wanted to make it quite clear that the good work he was doing in leaving money to help the poor was not done with any expectation that this would help towards his salvation, but rather 'because it will relieve them'. Butler explicitly rejected the traditional Catholic teaching that good works were meritorious. Like the small but growing number of Reading folk who owned and read Foxe's *Book of Martyrs*, or who organized Bible readings and prayers for their households, he was among those we can be fairly sure had been converted to the reformed religion.

Rather more certain than the religious beliefs of its citizens is the physical appearance of Reading in Tudor and Stuart times. The first known map of the town was drawn by John Speed in 1610 as part of

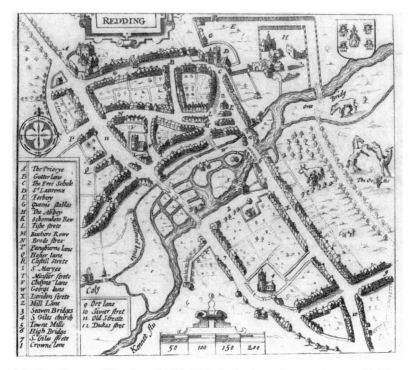

John Speed's map of Reading of 1610. This clearly shows the street layout, which has generally survived despite some major changes, especially to the line of the Kennet and the addition of eastern exits from the town

his series of county maps: *Theatre of the Empire of Great Britain*. Reading should have been included on the map of Berkshire, but the space was needed for a panoramic display of Windsor Castle. Since it was too important a town to be omitted, Speed found a spare corner on his map of Buckinghamshire for this the chief town of Berkshire! As he put it, 'For that Barkshire cold not contayne place for this Towne I have here inserted it as one of ye most ancient and chiefest in ye countye.'

Speed's plan shows the familiar 'Y' shape crossed by the many streamed Kennet. John Leland, writing in the reign of Henry VIII, had described the course of this river 'whereof the principal stream cometh through a great wood bridge in the south side of the town' with 'diverse armlettes breaking out . . . over which be diverse bridges of wood'. He especially noted its importance for the town's cloth industry.

The main settlement lay to the north of the Kennet along the streets between the long-disused Saxon market and the new market outside the abbey, where the stocks, the pillory and the well stood. Shoemaker Row, which bordered the market-place to the east, was still dominated by shoemakers: a survey of 1584 named eleven such craftsmen out of a total of seventeen. At the north end of the row, by the entrance to the abbey through the Compter Gate, was the house occupied in the 1590s by the mayor's sergeant, William Crissleton. He delivered all the mayor's writs but also plied the trade of a currier.

Along the streets were the houses of Reading's craftsmen which in many cases were also their workplaces. Each house stood on a long

A woodcut of an inn. In the sixteenth century Reading had several good inns, which were used not only by travellers but also by the townsfolk. Probate inventories of innkeepers show that some kept very comfortable establishments well supplied with local beer and even wine

narrow plot, with its back serving as yard, garden and allotment. Pigs and horses would be stabled there, cloth stretched out on racks, wood stored, and peas and beans grown. Occasionally fruit trees were grown and remembered with affection: when William Elkyns of Castle Street made his will in 1639, he said his wife should have the use of the 'court where cherry trees stand'.

In a town so permeated by the countryside, the smell of manure, piled in heaps in front of doors before being carted to the Forbury (the town midden), mingled with that of the brewers', tanners' and dyers' effluent. This poured into the Kennet along with the waste from the privies and hogsties, some of which also drained into the Holy Brook, even though this provided some of the town's water supply. Of course, none of this appears on Speed's very sanitized map, but it was a reality in 1610 and for many years afterwards. We know this from the frequent attempts by the corporation in the town's Court Leet to keep the streets and water supply clean by fining offenders, apparently without much effect.

The map shows clearly the three parish churches. St Laurence's, with its new churchyard, was the 'official' church of the town, with a special seat in the chancel for the mayor. Everyone else was seated in order of rank, the wealthiest at the front paying 1s. a year for a seat, and the ordinary folk at the back paying 1d. Here in the early seventeenth century the council and one person from every household assembled every Tuesday to hear an uplifting sermon or lecture. St Laurence was also the wealthiest parish. Many of its parishioners were mercers and clothiers: in 1524 to 1525 they paid nearly two-thirds of the total tax of the town. The parish of St Giles, which included the hamlet of Whitley, was always by far the poorest: it paid less in tax because it had more paupers and fewer wealthy tradesmen. St Mary's had about half the population of St Laurence's, but only about one-third of the wealth. A reference in St Mary's churchwardens' accounts notes that in 1573 its sexton, John Marshall, was paid to drive dogs out of the church. This may have given a little light relief to parishioners who found long sermons somewhat tedious.

From the registers of baptisms, marriages and burials kept in all three parishes comes our evidence for the occasional epidemics which interrupted the otherwise steady growth of the population. This rose from around 3,500 in 1540 to perhaps 6,000 by the Civil War. Epidemics occurred fairly regularly, though only in the case of bubonic plague was the cause ever stated in the registers. Plague was certainly in Reading between 1608 and 1609 (when 122 people, three times the normal yearly total, died from it in St Giles' parish), and again in 1625 and 1638. In the latter year 297 people died in the borough, about one in twenty of the population. This was despite measures taken to isolate victims in special houses on Whitley Hill and to inspect all dead bodies for signs of plague so as to isolate the family.

The same registers chronicle the early deaths of many babies, the accidental deaths of people drowned or run over by carts, and the criminals hanged in the county gaol. They also show up the long lives of Mistress Margaret Stevens, an aged midwife of eighty, and Mistress Alice Reeve, 'A good woman to the poor and in helping many of her neighbours with salve and oil of her own making without reward.'

Alice is also mentioned in her husband's will. The many hundreds of wills and their associated documents which survive, as well as other manuscripts produced by the church authorities, provide a rich store of evidence on the families, homes and work of Reading people in the sixteenth and seventeenth centuries. They remind us that four hundred years ago real people occupied the houses and walked the streets of the town – people with lives very different from our own, but with achievements, failures, joys and problems which we can appreciate.

Many of the townsfolk, perhaps two in every three, were not born in the town. These included people like Richard Tench, who was born in Shropshire, but came to Reading as a young man to work in the cloth industry. He married Alice, had at least four children and became a respected citizen as landlord of The Hind Head inn in

An early seventeenth-century woodcut of a family. The different roles of the husband and wife seem to be indicated by their positions: her caring for the children, him standing a little aloof. He smokes a pipe, a new fashion that was practised in Reading at this time.

London Street. He made friends, one of whom, William Dibley, worked with Tench as a young journeyman and remained close, visiting him in his last illness. Another was Thomas Kenton who left Henley-on-Thames as a teenager, became a baker in Reading and supplied The Hind Head with 'horsebread'. Richard was regarded by his friends as 'a good, sensible and wise man', though he never learned to write. Like some fathers Tench had trouble with his children, in this case his eldest son Richard, whose bad behaviour caused his father to reduce his inheritance. Other fathers had problems with daughters and occasionally sons over the choice of a spouse. Children were expected to defer to the better judgement of their parents in such matters, though it is clear they sometimes pleased themselves. For example, Humphrey Carter and Anne

Gunter went to Fawley early in the morning of St Valentine's day 1604, where they persuaded the minister to marry them.

Women were legally inferior: when single they owed obedience to their fathers, and on marriage all their possessions went to their husbands to whom they were subject. Yet in Tudor Reading, as elsewhere, they were often respected and loved. Some husbands took considerable care in their wills to ensure that they had a trouble-free widowhood. Henry Knight, a bell-founder, said his wife Elizabeth should have 'meat, drink, lodging, washing room, fire, fire candle and a chamber only to herself' (plus £4 a year to buy clothes), all in the house of her son Ellis and his wife. In other cases it seems that husband and wife were essentially partners in the family business,

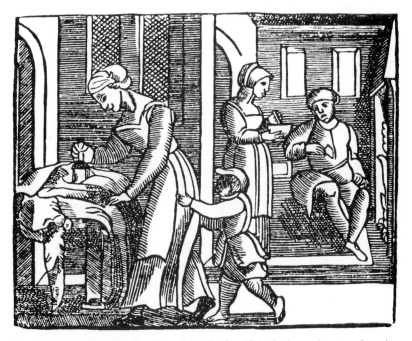

A composite woodcut showing the main work of a wife in the home: housework, caring for her children and ministering to her husband

A sixteenth-century German woodcut of a barber's shop. Probate inventories show that Reading had similar establishments where minor surgery, as well as hairdressing, was practised

which widows took over after the death of their spouses. Elizabeth Kent, who died in 1549, ran a cloth-making enterprise employing spinners and putting out work to weavers. She brought up her five daughters and married one of them into an important clothier family.

Given the way in which industry operated at this time, it is easy to see the importance of a husband-and-wife team. In order to practise a craft or trade a man had to serve an apprenticeship with a master who belonged to one of the four gilds into which the traders and craftsmen of Reading were organized. These were the mercers/drapers, the cutlers/bellfounders, the tanners/leather sellers and the clothiers/clothworkers. Smaller groups joined the cutlers' gild, which included such strange companions as carpenters, bricklayers, and barbers. The apprentice lived with the master's family, along with any unmarried young workmen who also had to be accommodated, making a small working community. Supervising the workers and selling their products occupied the husband; providing for the household took all the time and energy of the wife, who sometimes had a young girl to help her. Working as a servant in a town was attractive to country girls who could thereby earn some money to supplement or replace the 'marriage portion' from their fathers, and were also able to meet a wider selection of potential husbands than in the village. Not all of them were careful savers, however. One girl, Elizabeth Henwood, disarmingly confessed that she spent all she earned on new clothes.

Once his seven or more years of training were over, the apprentice was presented by his master to the town council for admission as a freeman. This meant he was free to practise his craft after the payment of a small entry fee, perhaps equivalent to three or four days' wages. Then he could be employed as a journeyman: the French origin of this term indicates that he was paid a 'daily' wage. Some apprentices would live with the family until they married. Their ambition was to become a master and have their own apprentices and journeymen, but few achieved this. In 1524 to 1525 half the taxpayers of Reading were wage-earners.

We can get some feeling for the working situation of Reading craftsmen from church court records. At about midday on a Tuesday in late November 1558 a quarrel developed in London Street. Thomas Buckland seized Joan Bateman as she walked down the street to her house in Butcher Row and pushed her into the 'canal', a gutter which would undoubtedly have been wet and dirty. Understandably she responded with some choice language, including the wish that he should be a cuckold all his life. Everyone in the tailor's workshop nearby seems to have watched the proceedings: Richard Bowen, the master aged about forty, who was upstairs in his loft cutting cloth; his eighteeen-year-old apprentice Thomas Robinson, down in the workshop; and his journeyman, twenty-four-year-old Thomas Walker, also an employee but living in a house he rented nearby. No one thought it unusual to down tools when something out of the

Many well-to-do traders and craftsmen in Reading possessed beds with curtains and feather mattresses, as in this seventeenth-century woodcut

ordinary happened. Everyone, men and women alike, worked long hours, but it was not the unremitting toil imposed by the later automatic processes in factories. The close-knit community, whose houses were at the same time homes, workplaces and shops,'was not without the problems associated with such confined living. Though private life was very difficult to keep private, and tempers, as we have seen, sometimes flared up into verbal and physical assaults on neighbours, there was always time to stand and stare.

Reading in the sixteenth and early seventeenth centuries was as much dependent on a single industry as, until a few years ago, Birmingham was on cars and Stoke on pottery. At least a third of all the craftsmen in Reading worked to produce cloth. The coloured cloths, 63 inches wide and 28–30 yards long, were as smooth as a billiard table and almost waterproof. They were prized both in England and in Europe. In 1606 Reading exported 5,753 broadcloths, more than six per cent of the national total. Kerseys, which were narrow, smaller and lighter than the broadcloths, were also made. The many processes involved in cloth production (except for carding and spinning the wool, which were done by women and children) were carried out by different groups of master craftsmen in their own workshops. These tasks were weaving, fulling (or thickening), dyeing and finishing.

The craftsmen were paid by the piece for the work they did by the clothiers, who were wealthy entrepreneurs or capitalists. It was they who bought the wool, organized its processing and then sold the final product to merchants, who exported it, usually from London. Often at least one process, either weaving or finishing, was carried out in the clothiers' own workshops, so that they were producers as well as merchants.

Concentration by historians on the central role of cloth production in the economy of Reading has often obscured the significance of other occupations. Important among these was the working of leather, at a time when shoes, clothing, harnesses and saddlery were made from this essential raw material. In 1584 there were eleven shoemakers in Shoemaker Row producing thousands of shoes a year to serve what must have been a very extensive local market. Just as all the shoemakers lived in St Laurence's parish, the glovers lived in St Mary's, while the tanners (whose trade produced obnoxious smells) were exiled to St Mary's or St Giles', where the Kennet provided the ample water supply they needed. Scattered through all three parishes were the carpenters, the joiners, the tallow chandlers and the cutlers, who provided for the everyday needs of the townsfolk. To buy food the housewife went to the market-place, where Butcher Row and Fisher Row housed retailers selling meat from the Berkshire villages, and fish from as far away as Newfoundland. Bakers could be found

The master shoemaker in this
sixteenth-century woodcut
employs two men who may be
journeymen or apprentices. The
workshop is also the 'retail' shop
where the customer is buying
readymade shoes

everywhere making different quality breads, the weight and price of
which were carefully controlled by the mayor. He and his officials also
controlled the quality of the fish, meat and beer sold in the town.

The price control of some essential commodities was very
important, especially in view of the inflation during the sixteenth
century which had a very damaging effect on wages. A growing
population in England produced a large pool of labour, which
contributed to a decline in real wages, and to an increase in poverty
and vagrancy. Reading had its share of these problems, and like other
towns attempted to keep out those poor or potential poor who drifted
into the town, by enforcing the law which ordered the whipping and
expulsion of vagrants. It also set up a house of correction, as we have
seen, at Greyfriars. Here the unemployed but able-bodied could be
set to work producing low-quality cloth, or dressing hemp and flax.
This would have contributed towards their keep but, more important,

would have cultivated industrious habits in those considered by the authorities to be tempted by idleness.

Nearly fifty years later a much more ambitious enterprise was set up under the terms of John Kendrick's will. A Reading man who made good in London as a cloth merchant, Kendrick died in 1624 without children. He left £7,500 to his birthplace to found a workplace where the poor could produce the fine-quality cloth for which Reading was well known. It was built in Gun Street on land sold by John's brother, William, to the council, and was later called The Oracle. It was constructed of bricks from Tilehurst and began operating in about 1628. It was demolished in 1850. Other less ambitious foundations survived rather longer, notably the almshouses founded by Sir Thomas Vachell in 1635 and rebuilt in the nineteenth century off Castle Street.

Sadly, by the time of Kendrick's charitable foundation, the cloth industry was in difficulties. Fashions were changing, and English

John Kendrick. This portrait (date unknown) used to hang in the Council Chamber in Reading

cloth no longer enjoyed such good sales in Europe, where wars made the situation even more difficult. So, too, did periodic outbreaks of plague in London, especially in 1625 when merchants fled and no cloth was sold. The town council, which controlled the quality of cloth, attempted to keep all the work in the industry within the town and to persuade rich clothiers to take on workers, but throughout the 1620s the problems of unemployment and underemployment continued. By 1633 the municipal corporation claimed that production was down by a third. Other areas in England were already experimenting with new kinds of lighter and more colourful woollen material which were becoming popular, but it seems that Reading paid insufficient attention to these new developments. Reading's cloth industry was well on the decline by the 1640s, though its final demise was a long time in coming.

Throughout the difficulties of the 1630s an extra problem had to be faced by Reading, as by other towns. This was the demand by King Charles I for taxes, especially ship money: it was his right to demand this, but many felt he was using it as a means to continue an unjust regime. Several men of Reading refused to pay the ship money tax and were distrained of goods. When the king finally agreed to call a parliament in 1640, there must have been many who saw this as the beginning of better times, but it was not so for Reading, at least not until somewhat later.

A date to be remembered in Reading was 1642. With the outbreak of the Civil War, the town found itself between King Charles's headquarters in Oxford and those of Parliament in London. Garrisoned first by several thousand royalist troops, successfully besieged by Parliament, drained by the taxation demands of both sides and the appalling loss of life among the citizens from disease, Reading suffered more than most towns in England. In a single year, 1643, an epidemic of typhus killed over five hundred people from only two parishes. The whole of Berkshire, which provided the customers for its markets and the raw materials for its industries

The Oracle, 1778. Nothing now remains of this building except for the gates, which are in the Museum of Reading

The interior of the Oracle, *c.* 1840. This water-colour by Henry Clarke Pidgeon shows the dilapidated state of the building in its last few years

An illustration from *A Dialogue or Parley between Prince Rupert's Dog Puddle and Tobie's Dog Pepper* (1642). This reflects the vicious character of the Civil War in which Reading was deeply involved for several years

(leather, grain and wool), was similarly affected by tramping armies, marauding troops and infectious disease.

For one of the town's most illustrious sons the conflict was fatal. William Laud, whose father was a cloth producer, had won one of the scholarships established at St John's College, Oxford, for boys from the borough. In 1633 he became Archbishop of Canterbury, the highest office ever attained by a Reading man. As a close adviser of Charles I and an advocate of religious policies unacceptable to many in Parliament, he was arrested and imprisoned before the war began and executed in 1643. Though some of its citizens disapproved of his ideas, Reading had cause to be grateful to him: in 1640 he gave the town lands worth £200 a year, the income to be used to apprentice poor boys and to give marriage portions to poor girls. There are still people in Reading who owe their early training as craftsmen to his benevolence.

Another important charity also began in the troubled times of the 1640s. Richard Aldworth, who died in 1646, left £4,000 to found a school for twenty poor boys. As with other similar foundations, the scholars were provided with a distinctive dress of blue, hence the name Bluecoat School. The original building, which was opened in 1660, stood at the junction of London Road and Silver Street.

Some Reading men, notably Tanfield Vachell and Daniel Blagrave, served on the parliamentary committee which ruled the county during and after the war. They eliminated from office such men as Anthony Blackston, a royalist supporter on the borough council. Anthony's nephew, the mayor, had earlier been kidnapped by royalist troops as a method of extorting yet more money from the reluctant citizens. One doubts whether many people cared greatly whether King or Parliament won; they just wanted the war to be over so that they could live their lives in peace. They were probably not aware that in July 1647 King Charles spent a few days with his younger children

Archbishop Laud
(date unknown)

The parliamentary army almost certainly improved the defences of Reading substantially after its capture in April 1643. This map is strangely orientated, north being at the bottom (Add MS 5415 E3)

at Caversham Park. He was in the custody of parliamentary troops, from whom he would later escape to begin a last futile attempt to regain power.

Though there was no fighting in Berkshire after 1646, the times were very unsettled. During the period of the Commonwealth (the rule of

Parliament and Oliver Cromwell), royalists lost their posts. They included the schoolmaster, Robert Jennings, the mayor, William Blackston (the kidnap victim), and the vicar of St Laurence's. The town rang its bells for Cromwell's victories over the future Charles II, and adopted a Presbyterian form of worship and church government. Even the town mace was deprived of its royal coat of arms and its cross.

However, with the restoration of the monarchy in the form of Charles II in 1660, the status quo was restored. Anglican clergy were reinstated; Presbyterian ministers were not only ejected from their parishes, but also forbidden to approach within five miles of them or to conduct religious assemblies other than those of the Church of England; the mayor and thirteen members of the corporation were dismissed and replaced by royalists; and the mace got back its royal coat of arms. At least the goldsmiths made a profit, for the town which had celebrated the successes of Cromwell now hastened to offer the new king fifty gold pieces when he came in 1663.

The same even-handedness to both sides in a conflict came in the 1680s. The corporation received King James II with great enthusiasm in 1685, only to show equal affection for William III in 1690, handing over the now much altered mace and forty broad pieces of gold in token of their obedience. How did the Vicar of Bray become so famous, when Reading had people just as able to survive all of these changes?

Much else was in a state of flux besides the political and religious affiliations of the corporation. The unsettling effects of the abolition of the monarchy and the bishops in the 1640s had encouraged the growth of radical religious groups. The tiny Baptist congregation in Reading in 1640 came out into the open during Cromwell's time. In 1655 George Fox, the founder of the Society of Friends (the Quakers), preached in the town, and he returned for an extended stay in 1658. Baptists, Quakers and Presbyterians refused to accept the Church of England after the restoration of the monarchy in 1660: under the harsh laws of the Cavalier Parliament, all were grouped together as non-conformists and penalized. Many found themselves in Reading Gaol, ironically on the site of what is now St Mary's in Castle Street. In 1688 John Bunyan came to Reading in secret; not until after the passing of the Toleration Act in 1689, following the accession of William III, could William Penn come to preach openly in the town.

By the 1690s the most far-reaching change of all had occurred in Reading. We have seen that the cloth industry was in difficulties in the early seventeenth century, and now in its closing years the future pattern of Reading's economy was becoming clearer. Gradually, but very definitely, the wealth of the town was moving from cloth-making to the malting of barley, to be sent to make beer for the ever-growing population of London.

By 1700 one in ten of the population of England lived in the capital, a vast market of half a million mouths to be fed, backs to be clothed and feet to be warmed. Berkshire and Oxfordshire supplied much of the wheat, barley and wood to feed and warm Londoners, and the merchants of Reading, with its wharves and Rivers Kennet and Thames, provided the means of getting these commodities to the customers. The leading men of the town, the mayors and councillors, were now as likely to be maltsters as clothiers. Indeed, it would seem that the richest men by this time were the maltsters, who used their capital to buy barley, and the roads and waterways converging on Reading to bring in the grain for malting. When Daniel Defoe came to Reading in 1724 he remarked on the once great cloth industry, but made much more of the one-hundred- and two-hundred-ton barges on the river and the great trade with London. Then, as now, Reading's transport links proved to be the key to its expansion and prosperity.

4

Reading in the Eighteenth Century and Victorian Times

TONY CORLEY

Though many relevant documents are available in the borough archives, the Berkshire Record Office and the Public Record Office in London, there has as yet been no systematic study of Reading in the eighteenth century which is based on this reference material. Therefore, we cannot be totally confident in offering answers to some basic questions, such as: how did the population of Reading and the wealth of the town grow during this period? Nevertheless, these are the sort of questions with which this chapter must deal.

In the preceding chapter it was estimated that Reading had a population of about 6,000 during the 1640s. For 1700, estimates based on the number of recorded baptisms and burials in the town produce a figure of around 7,000, while the 1801 census gives a more reliable figure of 9,770. So it looks as if there was a growth rate of around 17 per cent between 1640 and 1700 (which is equivalent to 28 per cent for the seventeenth century as a whole), and just under 40 per cent between 1700 and 1801. This compares with an estimated growth of 47 per cent for the county of Berkshire during the eighteenth century.

How wealthy did Reading become? The Poor Law rate was not introduced until after 1757; any assessments of rateable values are as yet still hidden in the borough records; and the parish rate books themselves are both very patchy and full of inconsistent valuations, so

Reading from the south, *c.* 1885. In the foreground are St Giles' church (left), a water tower (centre) and Christ Church (right). On the skyline are, left to right: the Town Hall, St Laurence's church, St James's (RC) church, the prison and the chimneys of Huntley & Palmers

that they cannot be relied on. We are therefore left with narrative rather than statistical evidence, but even so, this enables us to draw an instructive picture of the town in this period of its history.

Eighteenth-century Reading had two prominent characteristics: it was a prosperous market town, and its main industrial activity was malting. As a market situated in the west of Berkshire, which was a largely rural area (and in fact remained unspoilt until the Second World War), it dealt with agricultural produce of many kinds. Reading had two markets each week, which were supplemented by a series of annual fairs. This regular cycle of events not only provided a livelihood for the traders themselves, but also gave employment to shopkeepers, such as seedsmen, mealmen and purveyors of consumer goods, and to professional people such as solicitors and bankers. This last group was kept especially busy on market days.

As a trading centre Reading benefited greatly from its excellent communications. It was situated on a direct route between London and the West Country at a time when Bristol was still England's second city. The route between north and south was less close to the town: this linked Southampton with Oxford and the Midlands (a line followed by the modern A34), and ran through Newbury. Nevertheless, in an era when roads were generally poor, Reading had the supreme advantage of being only a mile or so from a different kind of major highway, the River Thames, and the town's increasing prosperity during the eighteenth century was closely bound up with successive improvements in its water transport.

In 1723 the River Kennet was made fully navigable as far as Newbury, which helped to open up the west of the county. From 1772 onwards the Thames navigation was steadily improved, so that barges carrying a hundred tons or more could be used. During the following two decades key canals were completed: the Thames and Severn Canal (1789) gave access to other waterways leading to Shropshire and Wales, and the Oxfordshire Canal (1790) provided a route to the Midlands and the north of England, where the Industrial Revolution was getting under way.

One important fact about the industrial revolution was that it gave the ordinary consumer the opportunity to buy inexpensive goods, from textiles to pots and pans. For the people of Reading, metal products of all kinds came down from Birmingham, pottery from Staffordshire, groceries from London, and stone from Bath – such as that used for the houses in Eldon Square. In return the town sent out agricultural produce: flour (twenty-thousand sacks a year in 1802), dairy produce, wool, malt, and especially timber.

The Kennet and Avon Canal, which connected Reading with Bristol and also the lower Severn Valley, was fully opened in 1810. By 1835, when Reading had 17,000 inhabitants, some 50,000 tons of goods were moving in and out of the town. Of this total, only 100 tons went by road, the rest by water. Coal imports totalled about

7,000 tons, much of this coming from the Midlands via the Oxfordshire Canal. Even in the 1850s, when rail transport was beginning to compete with the waterways, biscuits from Huntley & Palmers and agricultural machinery from the Reading Iron Works often travelled to the heart of England by canal. As late as 1870 the ironworks received large quantities of coal from the Somerset coalfields via the Somerset Coal Canal, which connected with the Kennet and Avon.

Besides its general importance as a market, Reading built up a very significant trade in malting. Earlier we saw that the staple industry of the town was cloth-making, but that was in terminal decline by the end of the seventeenth century. By 1760 Berkshire had become the most important area in England and Wales for malting, producing nearly 15,000 tons, over 5 per cent of the national total. Although malting also took place in towns like Abingdon and Wallingford, which were more immediately accessible to the barley-growing uplands of the county, it was Reading which sent the largest quantities of malt to the great London breweries of Truman, Whitbread and Barclay Perkins. These breweries, which between 1750 and 1800 doubled their output of beer from 400,000 to 800,000 barrels a year, did not have the space to carry out their own malting. Their requirements of malt would therefore have risen from 1,200 to 2,000 tons a year; not all of this came from Berkshire, but certainly large deliveries were taken downstream in capacious barges.

This malting activity was to be significant for Reading for two reasons. First, it earned the town a regular and considerable income: in 1790 five maltsters were rich enough to be entitled to vote. Second, it created wealth which was to have long-term implications for the industrial future of Reading. For example, Binfield Willis, a Quaker maltster who died in 1782, owned a large malthouse and other property in the town centre. His heiress, Mary, married Joseph Huntley, who used some of her money to set up the Huntley biscuit shop in London Street in 1822. Another example is William

VOL. I.   Numb. **1.**

Monday *July* 8, 1723.   (*To be continued Weekly.*)

READING:

Printed by · W. PARKS, and D. KINNIER, next Door to the *Saracen's-Head*, in *High-street* : Where all manner of Printing Bufinefs is handfomely done, as Books, Advertifements, Summons, Subpœnas, Funeral-Tickets, &c   Shop keepers Bills are done here after the beft manner, with the Prints of their Signs, or other proper Ornaments.   Alfo Gentlemen may have their Coats of Arms, or other Fancies curioufly cut in Wood, or engrav'd in Mettal.

[Price of this Paper, Three-Half-Pence per Week]

The front page of the first issue of Reading's earliest newspaper, showing a view of the town

Simonds, who came of a large landowning family in east Berkshire. After receiving a legacy of £550 from his father, he moved to Reading in the 1760s and began malting. As we shall see, the transition to Simonds Brewery followed in 1789.

The amenities, as would be expected in a medium-sized country town, were plentiful. From 1723 the *Reading Mercury* was published weekly. Its local news tended to be rather sparse until the 1800s, but the paper kept its readers in touch with what was happening in the wider world. From the middle of the eighteenth century there was an August race meeting on Bulmershe Heath, which culminated in a fashionable ball in the town hall. Until nearly the end of the century religious objections kept public theatrical performances out of the town, but in 1788 a theatre, with a short autumn season of a month or six weeks, was opened in Friar Street. On the other hand, musical concerts must have been regular events, for we hear of performances of works by Bach, Handel and others in 1774, and in 1786 when the new town hall was opened.

Reading was the location for some noteworthy schools. The free grammar school in the Forbury had a succession of able headmasters in the eighteenth century, thus attracting sons of the Berkshire gentry and also of some noblemen, who were repelled by the brutality of the regime at Eton. Dr Richard Valpy reigned as head for a record number of years – from 1781 to 1830. Although notorious as a mighty flogger, who whacked boys first and asked questions later, he was in other respects an enlightened man. Dr Valpy sought to instil into boys a liking for English literature, at a time when this subject was poorly taught elsewhere, and he regularly produced plays in English, Latin and Greek which drew wide acclaim. Moreover, Dr Valpy encouraged outdoor pursuits such as swimming and rowing; he allowed the girls from the school next door to share some lessons; and he invited them to evening parties and dances with the boys. Given his fame and achievements, why did Reading School not become a great nineteenth-century public school, as others such as Rugby did?

Reading School in the Forbury during Dr Valpy's headmastership, 1816

The answer seems to be that Dr Valpy stayed on long after he should have retired, and his incompetent successors merely hastened the school's subsequent decline. By 1866 there were no boys left, but in 1871 the school was reconstructed on its present site in Erleigh Road.

The girls' academy in Valpy's time was the Abbey School, which held lessons in the Abbey Gateway (there was no connection with the present Abbey School, which adopted that name in 1905). The school had a remarkable headmistress, Sarah Hackett, who chose to go under the name of Mrs Latournelle. She has been described by a biographer of Jane Austen as a 'heavy woman with a cork leg who brewed tea, hung out washing, darned stockings and cheerfully assigned her girls two-to-a-bed'. Two of her pupils were Cassandra and Jane Austen, daughters of a Hampshire clergyman. He had been a fellow of St John's College, Oxford, and was thus well aware of a connection between Reading School and the founder of the college, Sir Thomas White. The Austen girls spent eighteen months at the

Abbey School in 1786–7; while the elder was chattering with other pupils or with boys during the long afternoons when the headmistress left them to their own devices, Jane, the gawky and shy ten-year-old, kept her nose in her books. She had a retarded, deaf-and-dumb brother, so that she did not have Dickens's relish for physical deformities, but perhaps Mrs Latournelle survives in some of her good-natured but trivially minded women such as Mrs Allen in *Northanger Abbey*.

There are many signs that efforts were being made in the late-eighteenth century to improve the quality of life in Reading. Following a private Act of Parliament, the streets were better paved and lit; a mail coach service was introduced; the town hall was rebuilt in 1786 and the Reading Theatre was opened two years later; the High Bridge at the north end of London Street replaced an old timber bridge; and the two canals completed around 1790 (the Thames and Severn, and the Oxfordshire) helped to shift the main direction of Reading's communications away from London and towards some rapidly growing regions of Britain.

One important example of better infrastructure, essential to future progress, was the establishment, in 1788, of the first Reading bank, that of Marsh & Deane. It remains a mystery how money payments had been made earlier in the century, as the volume of commerce steadily expanded. We know that some prosperous maltsters in Abingdon had promoted the first bank in Berkshire in the previous decade. The larger Reading traders must often have had to manage with bills of exchange or IOUs, or perhaps notes issued by London banks: coins would have been too cumbersome and risky to transport in the volume needed for large transactions. Banks, with their correspondents in London and elsewhere, permitted the development of more complex financial dealings, while the waterways were encouraging wider-ranging trade.

The founder of the Reading bank, Sir Charles Marsh, had made a fortune in India; now he joined up with the Reading-born brewer and

William Blackall Simonds
(1761–1834), founder of
Simonds's Brewery in 1789

Receiver-General of Taxes for Berkshire, John Deane. Together they held large sums of money which they were able to use profitably. A further bank was established in 1791, with two brewers among the first partners. One of these was William Blackall Simonds, who had recently inherited his father's malting business and in 1789 had set up a new brewery, designed by his friend Sir John Soane, at Seven Bridges, now Bridge Street. A brewing cartel, which forced the thirsty citizens of Reading to drink inferior beer at exorbitant prices, was one of the more deplorable scandals of this period. This arose from the refusal of the town's magistrates to grant licences for new public houses. W.B. Simonds, anxious to supply good beer using his up-to-date technology – which from 1799 included a Boulton and Watt steam engine – became so disillusioned that he handed over the brewery to his eldest son and withdrew from the bank, which was renamed Stephens Blandy & Co, and in the twentieth century

A banknote of the 'new' Reading Bank, founded by W.B. Simonds in 1814 (now Barclays Bank, Market Place)

became part of Lloyds Bank. W.B. Simonds founded a new Simonds Bank, which was later absorbed into Barclays Bank. The brewery itself was unable to make much headway until the Beer Act of 1830 allowed new outlets to be established, finally leading to the destruction of the earlier cartel.

Another Reading entrepreneur who responded to the needs of an increasingly affluent market was James Cocks, who in 1789 started business as a fishmonger. In 1802 he began to manufacture a sauce, which was soon being conveyed, mainly by canal, to every major town and city in Britain: some even went overseas. He combined this activity with a delicatessen business, helping his cash-flow with sales of seafood and other provisions. Cocks's firm survived in Kings Road until 1962.

These civic and industrial innovations were speeded up by the external shock of the revolutionary and Napoleonic wars from 1793 onwards. As an inland town, Reading provided not only agricultural but also military supplies of many kinds. Musgrave Lamb's sailcloth factory, in Reading's industrial estate, manufactured so much sailcloth for the Royal Navy that the Battle of Trafalgar was said to have been won in Katesgrove Lane! The town raised its own militia and volunteers to repel a possible invasion, and it was host to refugees, including *émigré* Catholic clergy, and to French prisoners.

Geographically, Reading still remained in its centuries-old triangle, bounded by Friar Street to the north, Southampton Street to the west and London Street to the east – the latter two roads meeting at Whitley Cross. Reading was an urban area surrounded by farms and market gardens. While the better-off had reasonably roomy houses, the poorer inhabitants lived in overcrowded courts, usually hidden from the main thoroughfares. It is instructive to compare the census returns for 1841 with the town directory, which ignored about half of the households known to exist at that time.

Simond's Brewery from the River Kennet, *c.* 1850. The brewer's house, designed by Sir John Soane, is on the left, the malt houses on the right and St Mary's church behind

Cocks' Reading Sauce
Manufactory, Kings Road,
c. 1890. The Baptist chapel
is next door

Charles Morris (1834–99),
proprietor of Cocks' Reading
Sauce Manufactory (1873–99),
with his wife, Jessie Anne, the
daughter of Charles Cocks

Public health amenities were, on the whole, poor until the latter half of the nineteenth century, but in this respect Reading was little different from other country towns of great antiquity. Attempts from 1820 onwards to improve the water supply were only partly successful. A lack of drainage and sanitation spread disease and death, which in turn led to the churchyards being congested and themselves becoming a health hazard. Not until 1843 was a large new burial ground laid out at Cemetery Junction. The Reading Gas Company had been founded in 1818, and a new local government structure replaced the old torpid and unreformed corporation in 1835. In many ways Reading at the end of the eighteenth century continued to look backward to the Middle Ages, and the big move forward into the modern era was still to come.

The main events in Reading during the nineteenth century need not be narrated at such length as those of earlier times, since the story is readily available elsewhere. We can obtain a flavour of life in the town in the early part of this century by looking at John Man's *The Stranger in Reading: Letters from a Traveller to his Friend in London* (1810); Mary Russell Mitford's *Belford Regis, or Sketches of a Country Town* (1835); An Octogenarian [W.S. Darter]'s *Reminiscences* (1889); and W.M. Childs' *The Town of Reading during the Early Part of the Nineteenth Century* (1910). With the exception of the first, all these books have been reprinted in the last fifty years. *The Story of Reading* (1990) by Daphne Phillips has a number of informative chapters on this period, including discussions of the impact on Reading of both parliamentary and local government reform; the coming of the railways; the expansion of the town in Victorian times; nineteenth-century public health and welfare; and the significant events between 1870 and 1900. The remainder of this chapter will therefore concentrate on a subject which still deserves more study: the circumstances of the industrialization of Reading, and its effects on the economy, and the national and international reputation of the town.

John Sutton (1777–1863),
founder of Sutton & Sons,
seedsmen

The new century effectively began for Reading with the conclusion of the Napoleonic Wars. Having enjoyed great prosperity during the wartime agricultural boom, Reading was badly hit by the ensuing slump. In January 1815 Marsh & Deane's Bank failed, partly through poor management and over-reliance on personal loans. Among those worst affected were the Sutton brothers, one a miller and one a mealman. The younger brother, John, was able to continue with a much-reduced flour and meal business. It was left to his son, Martin Hope Sutton (1815–1901), to diversify into seeds and grasses, at a time when not only farmers and gardeners on large estates, but also those with suburban gardens, were increasingly demanding seeds. After the penny post was introduced in 1840, Sutton rapidly built up a lucrative mail-order business, sending out catalogues at the outset of the growing season and executing orders on the day of receipt. By 1900 the Suttons Seeds firm had extensive premises in the Forbury, trial grounds to the east of Reading, and an annual turnover of £216,000.

The pattern was now establishing itself: able entrepreneurs (usually born outside the town) taking advantage of Reading's good communications in order to set up businesses connected in some way with agriculture. Joseph Huntley's biscuit shop of 1822, using local flour, has already been mentioned. It was situated in London Street opposite one of Reading's two main posting inns, the Crown, and within two decades, it was marketing biscuits throughout much of southern England. Huntley's son Thomas ran the shop, and his other son, Joseph junior, who founded the later Huntley Boorne & Stevens, manufactured tins to keep the biscuits fresh in transit. Then, in 1841, Thomas took as a partner his cousin George Palmer, a Quaker like Huntley, whose ambition was to mechanize the making of biscuits. Achieving success in this aim by 1846, Palmer moved to a factory site near the Kennet. Huntley & Palmers soon made Reading famous throughout Britain and the world, producing nearly 25,000 tons of biscuits and cakes in 1900, with a turnover of £1,350,000. It was by far the largest employer in Reading, giving jobs to as many as 7,000, of whom 5,500 were employees in the factory.

Market Place, Reading, looking towards St Laurence's church (and piazza), 1856. Suttons' seed shop is third from right, next to the *Reading Mercury* office

Joseph Huntley (1807–95), founder
of Huntley Boorne & Stevens

Huntley Boorne & Stevens' tin works in London Street, shortly before the retail shop
closed, 1911

The construction of the railway in 1840, to link London with Bath and Bristol, helped to bring prosperity to a small foundry in Katesgrove Lane, from which materials were purchased locally. The foundry later became the Reading Iron Works, one of the largest suppliers of agricultural machinery in Britain with 360 employees. Though in the forefront of contemporary technology, especially steam engines, the iron works failed in 1887 through commercial incompetence, during the prolonged agricultural slump which had begun in the 1870s. But for this mismanagement, Katesgrove Lane might have added to its Trafalgar fame by later housing one of the most important engineering works in the south of England.

The Great Western Railway, and later its rival line which became the Southern Railway, also brought employment to Reading. Although it never became a railway town, as Swindon did thanks to its large-scale engineering workshops, Reading's workers employed

George Barrett (1771–1858) of Barrett Exall & Andrewes (later Reading Iron Works)

Barrett Exall & Andrewes' iron works (later Reading Iron Works), 1858

on the railways increased from 166 in 1861 to nearly 1,000 in 1901. Huntley & Palmers sent out by rail most of the 25,000 tons of biscuits and cakes it produced that year, and had its own sidings which connected with the various networks. Suttons likewise shipped its larger wholesale orders by rail. Although the canals continued for some decades to convey local goods traffic, their long-term demise as freight carriers was inevitable. Among other groups to be hit by the coming of the railways were the coaching inns such as The Crown. On the other hand the Great Western Hotel near the station, built in 1844, prospered for over a century and a quarter.

By 1851 the population of the borough was over 21,000 – more than twice that of 1801. Some entrepreneurs helped to build dwellings for their workers, as did the Palmers at Newtown and Norcot. Most building, however, was speculative, especially after the Crown Estate in eastern Reading was auctioned off in 1832–3, and Kings Road and Queens Road, named after William IV and Queen Adelaide, were laid out. The town was also expanding along the

Thomas Huntley (1803–57),
co-founder of Huntley & Palmers

George Palmer (1818–97),
co-founder of Huntley & Palmers

Oxford Road. In 1889 St George's parish to the west was incorporated in the borough, which by 1901 had a population of 72,000. Not until 1911 were Caversham and Tilehurst brought within Reading's boundaries.

After the 1840s the momentum of Victorian expansion was unstoppable. Some of Reading's most prestigious firms went on to become the leaders of their kind in Britain and sometimes even in the world. Well before the end of the century the biscuit firm of Huntley & Palmers was despatching its products from Reading to virtually every part of the globe: by 1914 it sent roughly half of its production overseas. Stories were common of explorers struggling laboriously to remote localities such as Tibet, previously unvisited by Westerners, only to be offered Huntley & Palmers' biscuits by local dignitaries. Suttons, too, made the name of Reading internationally famous through its exports, using airtight tins and other containers to keep

Sutton & Sons' extensive buildings in the Forbury, with the Market Place shop in the centre, 1890s

seeds in prime condition during the often lengthy voyages. Before its demise in 1887 the Reading Iron Works sent its engineering products to many distant lands. Less important goods also became celebrated overseas. Phileas Fogg, the hero of Jules Verne's *Around the World in Eighty Days* (1873), is portrayed as having daily breakfasted at the Reform Club in London on broiled fish garnished with Cocks's Reading sauce.

The Simondses had by 1900 one of the most extensive provincial breweries in the south of England. It was also very progressive, having one of the earliest laboratories in a brewery: it introduced a novel system of fermentation in the 1880s, and promoted pale ale and the less strong SB brew, as social improvements led to changed drinking tastes. It expanded considerably through being appointed supplier to military canteens, especially after Aldershot became the home of the army in the 1850s. That appointment led to overseas branches being set up in colonies such as Malta and Gibraltar. The brewery also secured contracts for railway refreshment rooms and bars on seaside piers.

Reading benefited immeasurably from exchanging its modest reputation as a market town for a renown which was not merely national but also worldwide. The goodwill which its main industries earned for the town encouraged smaller enterprises to try to bask in the reflected glory of Reading products. These included Serpell's and Meaby's in biscuits. Fidler and Oakshott & Millard in seeds, and Dymore Brown and the short-lived Berkshire Brewery in beer. Some other firms did well on a limited scale, such as the Castle and Mill Lane breweries, Wilder's and Williams's foundries, and, from 1901 onwards, the Pulsometer Engineering Company.

These firms, and many others which produced everything from bricks to bicycles, gave employment to thousands of townspeople, and indirectly to many more through shops and other secondary traders. But a town the size of Reading (72,000 in 1901) needed a variety of other workers to keep the wheels of wealth revolving. So, in addition to

Advertisement showing the original Huntley & Palmer's factory, a former silk mill, 1846. Note the steam train in the background

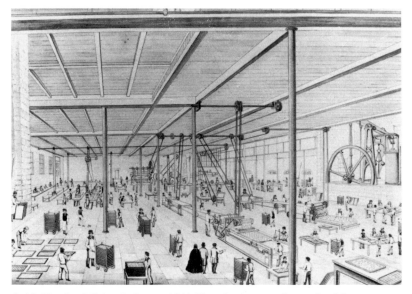

Inside Huntley & Palmer's factory, 1861. Note the steam engine on the right

the 7,000 at Huntley & Palmers and 2,000 at Suttons, the 1901 census reveals that in the borough there were over 3,000 construction workers, 1,600 professional people (including teachers), just over 1,000 general labourers, 990 employed in engineering, 980 on the railways, and no fewer than 920 coachmen, carters and others engaged in road transport. To later generations this last group may seem surprisingly numerous, but it would not have appeared so at the time to those braving the roads of Reading, which were congested with horse-drawn vehicles of all kinds. There were also 475 gardeners.

Apart from the professional groups, most of these workers were poorly paid. Even though most of the outlying farms and market gardens had been swallowed up by urbanization, Reading was still surrounded by an agricultural hinterland which, by deterring industrial mobility, helped to keep down wages. The largest employers, Huntley & Palmers and Suttons, paid their ordinary workers no more than £1 a

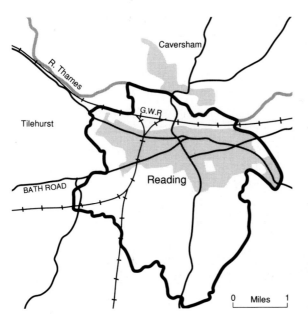

Reading at the end of the nineteenth century (bold line is borough boundary, shading is built-up area)

week, though there were opportunities for overtime during busy periods, such as before Christmas. Moreover, though Reading tended to have better-quality housing than many comparable towns, rents were high: up to 25 per cent of the earnings of an unskilled worker. Not surprisingly, therefore, population growth tended to be low, and the less affluent with large families suffered from want.

To some extent the personal benevolence of paternalistic nineteenth-century employers eased this burden, but a less caring entrepreneurial generation took over in the next century, and it was not long before industrial unrest came to a head. In the hot summer of 1911, when disputes were prevalent nationally, the workforce at Huntley & Palmers came out on strike for the first time over pay and trade union recognition. After some bluster the management responded with limited wage rises. Discontent was inflamed by the news that year that the virtual-millionaire Palmers were donating £150,000 to Reading University College, with no comparable gifts coming to benefit their own workers or the people of Reading. It took threats from the Liberal government about minimum wage orders in tin-making and other 'sweated' industries to force Huntley Boorne & Stevens, and subsequently Huntley & Palmers, to improve both wages and working hours. The latter opened a social centre in 1938.

The extent of economic deprivation was not revealed until 1912, when Professor Arthur Bowley of the University College carried out a household survey of the town , which was, incidentally, a major development in social research. Bowley's findings revealed that one in four working-class people, and one in five of all Reading families, were living in 'primary poverty' – receiving less than enough income to maintain reasonable physical health (as measured by the undemanding standards of those days). Nearly half of all children, both those in education and those below school age, fell into this category. Bowley rightly found these results to be 'shocking', since the poverty revealed was not intermittent but permanent, and a regular feature of the industries of Reading. 'To raise the wages of the worst-paid workers', he declared 'is the most pressing task with which the country is confronted today.' Labour shortages in the First World War did much to rectify this scandal of poor wages.

In the second and subsequent decades of the twentieth century, Reading was to undergo successive periods of adjustment: to a world war, to economic depression, to the Second World War, and to unprecedented changes of so many kinds since 1945. Just as important to the town as these adjustments have been the developments taking place in communications of all kinds, including easy access to a network of motorways and to Heathrow Airport.

Although, therefore, the borough of Reading in the 1990s contains about 130,000 inhabitants, many engaged in a variety of occupations from small-scale manufacturing to distribution and financial and computer services, it is now the centre of a very thriving conurbation, comprising well over double that number. Its national and international links, often with and through London, offer a promise of sustained economic prosperity well into the twenty-first century.

Bibliography

General

For further reading a number of works may be consulted, including:

Victoria County History of Berkshire 1906–27, especially Vols II and III.
Berkshire Archaeological Journal, various articles over the last century.
Coates, C. *The History and Antiquities of Reading* 1802.
Phillips, D. *The Story of Reading* (2nd end) 1990.

Daphne Phillips's book contains a bibliography, to which the interested reader is referred.

The following items are of particular relevance to individual chapters in this book:

Chapter 1

Whitelock, D. *The Anglo-Saxon Chronicle: a Revised Translation* 1961.
Berkshire Archaeological Journal articles over the last century have covered all archaeological discoveries relating to Reading.
Berkshire Sites and Monuments Record, maintained in the Planning Department of Berkshire County Council. This has details of all archaeological discoveries.

Chapter 2

Slade, C.F. 'Reading' in *Historic Towns* Vol. I (ed. M.D. Lobel) 1969.
Astill, G.G. 'Reading' in his *Historic Towns in Berkshire: an Archaeological Appraisal* 1978.
Hurry, J.B. *Reading Abbey* 1901.
Kemp, B.R. (ed) *Reading Abbey Cartulries* 2 Vols, Royal Historical Society, 1986–7.

Chapter 3

Barry, J. (ed) *The Tudor and Stuart Town 1530–1688* 1990.
Clark, P. & Slack P. (eds) *English Towns in Transition 1500–1700* 1976.
Dils, J. (ed) *Redding 1540–1640* 1980.
Goose, N. Decay and regeneration in seventeenth century Reading', *Southern History* 6, 1984.

Chapter 4

Alexander, A. *Borough Government and Politics: Reading 1835–1985* 1985.
Corley, T.A.B. *Quaker Enterprise in Biscuits: Huntley & Palmers of Reading 1822–1972* 1972.
Corley T.A.B., various articles on Reading industries in *Berkshire Archaeological Journal* from Vol. 66 (1971) onwards.
Naxton, M. *The History of Reading School* 1986.
Victoria County History of Berkshire 1906–27 Vol. II.
Yeo, S. *Religion and Voluntary Organisations in Crisis* 1976.

Index

abbey, *see* Reading Abbey

Abbey Gateway, 89

Abbey School, 89

abbot, 42, 49

abbot's bailiffs, 50, 51

Abingdon, 7, 50, 86, 90

Aclea, battle of, 16

Adam, Abbot, 40

Adelaide, Queen, 100

Adeliza, Queen, 36

Æthelbald, King, 7

Æthelwulf, ealdorman, 8, 17, 18

Æthelwulf, King, 7, 16

Agilbert, Bishop, 13

Aldershot, 103

Aldworth, Richard, 79

Alfred, King, 7, 8, 18, 20, 21

Anglo-Saxon Chronicle, 16, 21

Anscher, Abbot: hospital for lepers, 36

apprenticeship, 70, 74

Ashdown, battle of, 18, 20

Austen, Cassandra and Jane, 89

bailiffs, *see* abbot's bailiffs

Baptist chapel, Kings Road, 94

Baptists, 81

barges, 82, 85, 86

Barrett, George, 99

Barrett Exall & Andrewes, 99, 100; *see also* Reading Iron Works

Basing, battle of, 18

Bateman, Joan, 71

Bath, 10, 85, 99

Battle (Reading), 3

Battle Abbey (near Hastings), 28, 29

Bayeux Tapestry, 15, 23, 26

Bearroc, 8

Becket, Thomas, 34

Beer Act, 92

Benedictines, 33, 35, 38

Bensington, battle of, 7

Bere Court, 52

Berkshire, 7, 8

Berkshire Brewery, 103

Berkshire Record Office, 83

Birmingham, 85

Blackston, Anthony, 79

Blackston, William, 79, 81

Blagrave, Daniel, 79

Blagrave, John and Agnes, 58, 60

Blanche of Lancaster, 37

Blessed Virgin Mary, devotion to, 38

Bluecoat School, 79

borough of Reading, 23, 24, 25, 27, 30, 57, 107

Bowen, Richard, 71
Bowley, Professor Arthur, 106
Bridge Street, 91
bridges, 57
Bristol, 85, 99
Broad Street, 30
broadcloths, 73
Buckland, Thomas, 71
Bulmershe, manor of, 58
Bulmershe Heath, 88
Bunyan, John, 82
burgesses, 50, 51, 52, 57
Burghfield, 5
burgus, 32
burh, 21, 22
burial ground, 95
Butcher Row, 71, 73
Butler, Edward, 56, 57, 58, 63
Butts, 10, 44

Cadel, *Cadelsgroue*, 29
canals, 85, 86, 90, 100
Carter, Humphrey, 68
castle, 26
Castle Brewery, 103
Castle Hill, 26
Castle Street, 26, 66, 75, 82
Caversham, 1, 17, 29, 102
Caversham Park, 80
Cemetery Junction, 95
census of 1801, 83
census of 1901, 103
ceorls, 11
Charles I, 59, 76, 78, 79
Charles II, 82
charter, 57, 59

chepyngavell (or *Chepinggavel*), 24, 51
Childs, W.M., 95
Christ Church (Reading), 84
Christianity, coming of, 13
church (early buildings), 10, 13, 14
church court records, 71
Civil War, 76, 78
clergy, 13
clothiers/clothworkers, 70
cloth-making, cloth industry, 62, 65, 70, 72–3, 75–6, 82, 86
Cluny, Cluniac monasticism, 33, 35
Cnut (Canute), 21, 22
Cocks, James, 92
Cocks' Reading sauce, 92, 94, 103
cofferers, 57
Coley, 29
Commonwealth, 80
communication, routes of, 1, 2, 10, 11, 16, 31, 85, 97, 107
constables, 51
cotsetlas, 12
Court Leet, 66
craft guilds, 48
Crane Wharf, 3
Crissleton, William, 65
Cromwell, Oliver, 81
Cromwell, Thomas, 53, 58
Crown Estate, 100
Crown inn, 97, 100
cutlers/bellfounders, 70

Danegeld, 16, 21
Danes, 15–22
Danish camp, Danish occupation, 9, 17, 18, 19, 20, 29

Darter, W.S., 95
de Ferrers, Henry, 27, 28
Deane, John, 91
Defoe, Daniel, 82
Dibley, William, 68
Domesday Book, 6, 27, 28, 29, 31
Dorchester-on-Thames, 13
drapers, 48
Dreadnought, 4
Duke Street, 56
Dymore Brown, 103

ealdorman, 7
Earley, 27, 29
East Anglia, 16
Edward IV, 37
Edward VI, 56, 62, 63
Edward the Confessor, 22, 23, 24
Egbert, King, 7, 16
Eldon Square, 85
Elizabeth I, 57, 62, 63
Elkyns, William, 68
Ellandune, battle of, 7
Englefield, battle of, 18
epidemics, 61, 67, 76
Erleigh Road, 89
Ethelræd II (Unræd), 21

fairs, 48, 61, 84
Faringdon, Abbot Hugh Cooke,
    52–3, 55, 56
Fawley, 69
Fidler's seeds, 103
Fisher Row, 73
Fobney, 29
food rents, 12

Forbury, 30, 66, 88, 89, 96, 102
Fox, George, 81
Foxe's *Book of Martyrs*, 63
Friar Street, 46, 58, 88, 93

geburs, 12
geld, 21
Germanic cemeteries, 3
Germans, 3
gesiths, 12
gild, stewards of, 50
gild hall, 61
gild merchant, 50, 51
gilds, 70
Godric, 27
Goring Gap, 17
grammar school, 61; *see also*
    Reading School
Great Western Hotel, 100
Great Western Railway, 19, 99
Grey, Agnes, 60
Grey, William, 58, 62
Greyfriars, 58, 61, 74
Gun Street, 10, 75
Gunter, Anne, 69

Hackett, Sarah (Mrs Latournelle), 89
Hastings, battle of, 25
heathenism, 14
Henry I, 31, 33, 36, 44, 48
Henry II, 36, 39, 48
Henry III, 35, 42
Henry VI, 51
Henry VII, 51
Henry VIII, 31, 52, 56, 62, 63, 64
Henwood, Elizabeth, 71

High Bridge, 18, 30, 90
Hind Head inn, 67, 68
Hingston Down, battle of, 16
Hocktide, 63
Holy Brook, 18, 29, 66
Horn Street, 10
hospital, 61
house of correction, 61, 74
Hugh II, Abbot: hospital for the
    poor and pilgrims, 36
Hugh of Amiens, 33
hundred of Reading, 5, 6
Huntley, Joseph, 86, 97
Huntley, Joseph, jnr, 97, 98
Huntley, Thomas, 97, 101
Huntley Boorne & Stevens, 97, 98,
    106
Huntley & Palmers, 84, 86, 97, 100,
    101, 102, 103, 104, 105, 106

Icknield Way, 6, 17
Immaculate Conception, cult of, 38
industrial unrest, 106
industrialization, 95ff.
infant mortality, 11
influenza, 61

Jack of Both Sides inn, 3
James II, 81
Jennings, Robert, 81
John, Count, later King, 40, 48
John of Gaunt, 37
journeyman, 71, 74

Katesgrove, 29
Katesgrove Lane, 93, 99

Kendrick, John, 75
Kendrick, William, 75
Kennet, river, 1, 17, 29, 31, 58, 61,
    64, 65, 66, 73, 82, 85, 97
Kennet and Avon Canal, 85, 86
Kennet Mouth, 3, 4, 10
Kent, Elizabeth, 70
Kent, Thomas of Southcote, 62, 63
Kenton, Thomas, 68
kerseys, 73
Kings Road, 92, 94, 100
Knight, Henry and Elizabeth, son
    Ellis, 69

Latournelle, Mrs, *see* Hackett
Laud, William, 78, 79
leather working, 73
Leicester, 13
Leland, John, 64
Leveva, Abbess, 28, 29
Lewes, 33
Londinium, 1
London, Dr (commissioner), 58
London, 10, 24, 73, 76, 82, 85, 107
London breweries, 86
London Road, 79
London Street, 68, 71, 86, 90, 93,
    97, 98
lordship of Reading, 56

mace, 51, 81
Malmesbury, William of, 36
malting, 82, 84, 86
Man, John, 95
manor of Reading, 9, 12, 13, 28,
    35, 57

manorialism, 12
market, 11, 14, 44, 48, 61, 65, 84
Market Place, 73, 97, 102
Marsh, Sir Charles, 90
Marsh & Deane's bank, 90, 91, 96
Marshall, John, 66
Mary, Queen, 63
Matilda, Queen, 39
mayor, 51, 52, 56, 57, 61, 66, 74, 79, 81
mayor's sergeant, 65
Meaby's biscuits, 103
mercers/drapers, 70
Mercia, 7, 13, 16, 17
Meretun, battle of, 18
Middle Saxons, 7
Mill Lane, 30
Mill Lane brewery, 103
minster church, 13, 29
Minster Street, 13, 29
mint, 23, 24
Mitford, Mary Russell, 95
Montacute, 22
Morris, Charles, 94
Musgrave Lamb's, 93

name of town, 3, 5
Napoleonic Wars, 92, 96
New Market, 30
New Street, 30, 46
Newbury, 85
Newtown, 100
Nicholas, Abbot, 45
Norcot, 100
Norman Conquest, 25–7
Northumbria, 16

Nottingham, 17
nunnery, 29

Oakshott & Millard, 103
Offa, King, 7
Oracle, The, 75, 77
Oxford, 10, 76, 85
Oxford Road, 1, 102
Oxfordshire Canal, 85, 86, 90

Palmer, George, 97, 101
Palmer family, 100, 106
Pangbourne, 6
parish gilds, 63
parliamentary troops, 76
Penn, William, 82
Peter, Prior, 33
Phillips, Daphne, 95, 108
pillory, 65
plague, 11, 15, 61, 67, 76
plays, 63
Pons, Abbot (of Cluny), 33
population of Reading, 11, 29, 67, 83
Portmanbrook, 29
Portmanbrook meadow, 51
poverty, 106
Presbyterians, 81
prison, see Reading Gaol
Prospect Park, 26
public health amenities, 95
Public Record Office, 55, 83
Pulsometer Engineering Company, 103

Quakers, 81
Queens Road, 100

rail transport, 86
railway, construction of, 99
Reada, 5
Reading, University College of, 106
Reading Abbey, abbey church, 29; abbot, 42, 49, *see also* Adam Anscher, Faringdon, Hugh II, Nicholas; archaeological finds, 3; architecture, 40; artistic importance, 37; cellarer's range, 35; chapter house, 35, 53, 54; Compter Gate, 46, 48, 65; conflicts with town, 50, 51; dedication, 34; destruction, 56; dissolution, 52, 56; *domus necessaria*, 35; dormitory, 35; economic benefits to town, 46; establishment, 31; fairs, 48; floor tiles, 41, 44; hand of St James, 39–40; hospital, 36; hospitality, 36; hospitium, 61; impact of dissolution, 57; impact on town, 44ff; kings as patrons, 36; kings as visitors, 36, 37, 47, 57; Lady Chapel, 34; lordship of town, 49ff; Main Gate, *see* Reading Abbey, Compter Gate; markets, 48; mausoleum, 33; miracles, 39–40; 'mitred' abbey, 42; music, 41; 'parliamentary' abbey, 37, 42, 47; pilgrims, 36, 39, 46, 48; refectory, 35; relics, 39, 48; religious importance, 37; royal abbey, 33; ruins, 53, 54; seals, 38, 42, 45; servants, 47; statues, 41, 42; visitors, 37, 47; wealth, 61

Reading Bank, *see* Marsh & Deane, Simonds' Bank
Reading Gaol, 82, 84
Reading Gas Company, 95
Reading Iron Works (Barrett Exall & Andrewes), 86, 99, 100, 103
Reading Mercury, 87, 88, 97
Reading Museum and Art Gallery, 39, 41, 77
Reading School, 88–9
Reading Theatre, 88, 90
Readingas, 5
Reeve, Alice, 67
Reginald, Earl of Cornwall, 36
registers, parish, 67
Reinbald, 27, 28
relics, *see* Reading Abbey
religious practice, changes, 62
revolutionary wars, 92
Richard, Earl of Cornwall, 36
Richard I, 40
roads, road junctions, *see* communications
Robinson, Thomas, 71
Roman period, 1, 2, 3
royal status of Reading, 12–13, 17, 23, 31, 56

St Augustine, 13
St Birinus, 13
St George, parish, 102
St Giles, church and parish, 62, 66, 67, 73, 84
St James, 39, 45; cult of, 39; hand of, 39–40; Fair, 48
St James (RC) church, 84

St John the Evangelist, 38, 45
St John's College, Oxford, 78, 89
St Laurence, church and parish, 46, 48, 49, 56, 58, 60, 61, 62, 63, 66, 73, 81, 84, 97
St Laurence's Fair, 48
St Martin of Battle, Abbey of, 28
St Mary, 38
St Mary, church and parish, 29, 47, 57, 62, 66, 73, 93
St Mary's church, Castle Street, 82
St Pancras, Priory of, 33
St Philip, head of, 40
St Philip and St James the Less, Fair, 48
Saxon cemeteries, 4, 5
Saxons, 6
schools, 57, 61, 88
scot, 14
Serpell's biscuits, 103
Seven Bridges, *see* Bridge Street
Seymour, Edward, 56
Seymour, Queen Jane, 52
ship money, 76
Shoemaker Row, 65, 73
Silchester, 1, 3, 10
Silver Street, 79
Simonds, William Blackall, 88, 91, 92
Simonds' Bank, 92
Simonds' Brewery, 88, 91, 93, 103
slaves, 11
Soane, Sir John, 91, 93
Somerset Coal Canal, 86
Southampton, 10, 85
Southampton Street, 93
Southcote, 3, 60, 62

Southern Railway, 99
Speed, John, 63, 64, 66
Staffordshire, 85
Stamford Bridge, battle of, 25
Stephen, King, 34, 39
Stephens Blandy & Co., 91
Stevens, Margaret, 67
stocks, 65
Sumer is icumen in, 41, 43
Surrey, 7, 16
Sutton, John, 96
Sutton, Martin Hope, 96
Sutton & Sons, *see* Suttons Seeds
Suttons Seeds, 96, 97, 100, 102, 103, 105

tanners/leather sellers, 70
Tench, Richard and Alice, son Richard, 68
Thames, 1, 3, 6, 7, 10, 17, 18, 25, 31, 82, 85
Thames navigation, 85
Thames and Severn Canal, 85, 90
Theale, 6
thegns, 12
Thetford, 17
Tilehurst, 75, 102
Toleration Act, 82
Tothill, 29
Tovi, 21
town hall, 61, 88, 90
transport links, *see* communications
tun-gerefa, 12
typhus, 76

understeward, 56

Uniformity and Supremacy, Acts of, 63
Vachell, Tanfield, 79
Vachell, Thomas, 56, 58
Vachell, Sir Thomas, 75
vagrancy, 74
Valpy, Dr Richard, 88, 89
Vastern Road, 29
Vikings, *see* Danes
vill of Reading, 13, 23
vintners, 48

Walker, Thomas, 71
Wallingford, 8, 10, 23, 24, 25, 29, 86
Waltham, 22
Waltham Holy Cross, 22
Wantage, 7
warden (*custos*) of the gild, 51
water transport improvements, 85
well, 65

Wessex, 7, 13, 16, 17, 20, 21
West Saxons, 7, 17
Whitley, 29, 66
Whitley Cross, 93
Whitley Hill, 67
Wilder's foundry, 103
Wille, Henry, 50
William, son of Henry II, 36
William I, 25, 26
William III, 81, 82
William IV, 100
William of Normandy, *see* William I
Williams's foundry, 103
Willis, Binfield, 86
wills, 67
Wilton, battle of, 18
Winchester, 7, 10, 13, 17, 24
Wolvesey, Daniel, 50

York, 17